Praise for *Renewable*

"If you've ever felt despair about the st
'What can I do?' I recommend reading *Renewable*. Eileen Flanagan's insightful memoir shows a deep understanding of complex global problems, while showing us how one person can change their life while working to change the world we all share."

—**Kumi Naidoo**,
Executive Director of Greenpeace International

"In a book laced with humorous anecdotes, Eileen Flanagan writes of her quest for simplicity while beset by the contradictions of modern life. A former Peace Corps volunteer turned soccer mom, her dilemmas are easy to relate to, yet her narrative inspiring. The inner voice of integrity does point out a path all of us can follow."

—**George Lakey**,
author of *Toward a Living Revolution*

"A wise and delightful tale, reminding us not only of the need for simplicity but of the need to follow our heart's calling. The whole world benefits from those with the courage to do so."

—**Bronnie Ware**,
author of *The Top Five Regrets of the Dying*

"*Renewable*. A big, wonderful word, filled with faith and hope and goodness. And this is a big, wonderful memoir. Truly. There is a passage in the book where Flanagan describes seeing the play *Our Town*, by Thornton Wilder, and Emily, the play's lead, goes back to witness a day in her life—her twelfth birthday—and it's the moment—THE MOMENT in the play—when Emily realizes that the living don't know how precious life is. It's one of those heart-stopping, breathtaking moments when you're sitting in a dark theater and you get it. Reading this book was like that for me. This book, this big, wonderful book, will remind you of the very same thing—that life is indeed very, very precious. Eileen Flanagan is a courageous warrior, she is a courageous writer, and she is the very definition of goddess."

—**Amy Ferris**,
author of *Marrying George Clooney:
Confessions from a Midlife Crisis*

Praise for *The Wisdom to Know the Difference*

"*The Wisdom to Know the Difference* is about being able to change . . . What is important is that we can make a change and transform ourselves into better, happier people."

—**The Dalai Lama**

"Eileen Flanagan is a Quaker writer who you're going to hear a whole lot more about in coming years. She's just finding her voice nationally—and what a voice it is!"

—**David Crumm,**
editor and founder of *Read the Spirit*

"Eileen Flanagan is, quite simply, a superb nonfiction writer."

—**Rose Rosetree,**
Pathways Magazine

"Chock-full of Quaker wisdom and everyday stories that become parables in Flanagan's hands, this is one of those rare books that give us as readers permission to be—to fully and completely 'be.'"

—**Phyllis Tickle,**
author of *The Great Emergence*

"We've all heard 'grant me the serenity to accept the things I cannot change, and the courage to change the things I can,' but we rarely hear how to find the wisdom to know and act on the difference. Until now. This beautiful book weaves together fascinating stories and timeless wisdom from across spiritual traditions to create a practical map for all of us to navigate this very question."

—**Diana Winston,**
Director of Mindfulness Education at UCLA's
Mindful Awareness Research Center,
and co-author of *Fully Present:
The Science, Art, and Practice of Mindfulness*

"Eileen Flanagan effortlessly weaves the wisdom of the ordinary people she has met on her path with the extraordinary wisdom of many spiritual teachers into a rich tapestry. A thoroughly good read from beginning to end, I highly recommend this book to anyone seeking spiritual wisdom."

—**Karen Casey, PhD,**
author of *Each Day a New Beginning*

Renewable

Other Works by Eileen Flanagan

The Wisdom to Know the Difference:
When to Make a Change—and When to Let Go.
New York, NY: Tarcher/Penguin, 2009.

God Raising Us: Parenting as a Spiritual Path.
Wallingford, PA: Pendle Hill Publications, 2008.

Listen with Your Heart: Seeking the Sacred in Romantic Love.
New York, NY: Warner Books, 1999.

Renewable

One Woman's Search *for*
Simplicity, Faithfulness,
and Hope

Eileen Flanagan

SHE WRITES PRESS

Published 2015
Printed in Canada
ISBN: 978-1-63152-968-9
Library of Congress Control Number: 2014954701

For information, address:
She Writes Press
1563 Solano Ave #546
Berkeley, CA 94707

She Writes Press is a division of Spark Point Studio, LLC.

Map of Africa by Mike Morgenfeld.
Portions of this work appeared in similar form in "Africa, Appalachia,
and Arrest," Friends Journal, May 2013.

For Megan, Luke, Mopati, and Tshego

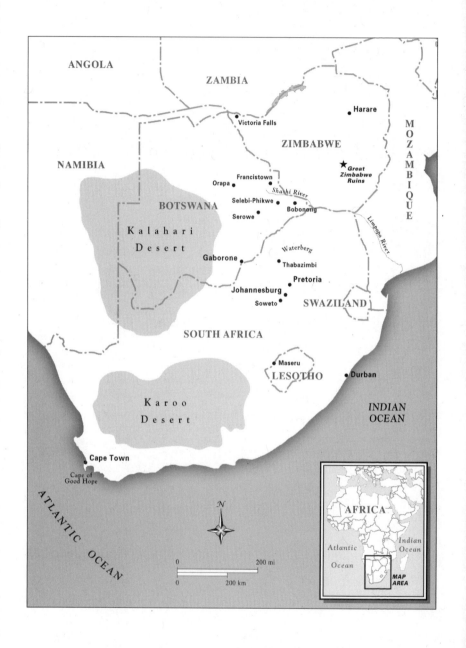

ANGOLA

ZAMBIA

NAMIBIA

Victoria Falls

Harare

ZIMBABWE

★ Great
Zimbabwe
Ruins

M
O
Z
A
M
B
I
Q
U
E

Orapa

Francistown

BOTSWANA

Selebi-Phikwe

Shashi River

Bobonong

Serowe

K a l a h a r i
D e s e r t

Waterberg

Gaborone

Thabazimbi

Limpopo River

Pretoria

Johannesburg

Soweto

SWAZILAND

SOUTH AFRICA

Maseru

LESOTHO

Durban

K a r o o
D e s e r t

INDIAN
OCEAN

Cape Town

Cape of
Good Hope

N

ATLANTIC OCEAN

0   200 mi

0   200 km

AFRICA

Atlantic
Ocean

Indian
Ocean

MAP
AREA

Contents

Preface:
A Good Day to Be Arrested

Ash Wednesday is a good day to be arrested.
—Reverend Jim Antal, United Church of Christ

A t age fifty, I snapped half a plastic handcuff around one wrought iron bar of the White House fence. Glancing over my shoulder at the famous sloping lawn and the imposing white pillars of the south portico, I slipped the other cuff around my maroon leather glove and locked it into place. To my left, Robert Kennedy, Jr. and his son Conor were doing the same. Beyond them stood civil rights icon Julian Bond and author Bill McKibben, whose books on global warming had helped lead me here to my first act of civil disobedience. In front of us, actress Daryl Hannah sat on the cold sidewalk by a banner telling President Obama to "Lead on Climate."

For me, a woman who had spent most of the past sixteen years identifying herself as a spiritual writer and mother of two, claiming a place in this company was actually more daunting than getting arrested by the DC Park Police, who stood behind the throng of reporters waiting to cart us away in police vans parked nearby. I had more experience carpooling to soccer games than standing in front of the press pool. At the training the night before, when Bill McKibben had told us to dress professionally and warmly, I realized I might not own the right wardrobe to do both, so I'd gone for warm. Now I felt slightly underdressed in my purple down coat and grey slacks as I glanced around at all the men wearing ties.

The two million–member Sierra Club had never authorized civil disobedience before, but both their board president and executive director were there, along with a top NASA climate scientist, a former poet laureate, and the US head of Greenpeace, who stood next to me. The impressive lineup was intended to attract attention to the action, which would be followed by a march of 40,000 people a few days later. The strategy was working. *The Philadelphia Inquirer* had already interviewed me about why a Philadelphia mother was concerned enough about global warming to go to jail, if only briefly.

How on earth had I gotten to this moment, willingly handcuffing my wrist to the White House fence with a bunch of famous people, while my family and friends back in Philadelphia prayed for me? Watching the press jostle for position in front of us, I almost laughed out loud, realizing how dramatically my life had changed in a little over a year.

Only the previous winter I had been preoccupied with our recent move into a five-bedroom house, unpacking the Irish and African history books I'd been carting around since graduate school, and waiting hours on hold for Verizon to transfer our phone and Internet service. Run ragged organizing multiple fundraisers for my son's seventh-grade trip to Costa Rica, I'd been drowning in e-mail, junk mail, and the unused kitchen gadgets the previous residents had left in our new basement. Sleepless at 3:00 a.m., I stared at the ceiling in a midlife hormonal funk and realized with a shock that my life was not what I had expected.

I thought of myself as a former Peace Corps volunteer who had loved living in a mud hut, and now I had more bathrooms than I could keep clean. I thought of myself as a person who used canvas shopping bags twenty years before it was mainstream, but now with two cars and two electronics-addicted teenagers, I'd developed a low-level despair about my inability to protect the planet they would inherit. I'd been reading about how global warming was withering maize crops in Botswana, the southern African country where I had taught decades earlier—the place that had originally taught me about social responsibility. Our new house was so big, no one heard me when I cried.

I had felt alone in my midlife angst, though I knew I really wasn't. I'd heard whispers from my middle-class friends, more than one of whom wished she had less house and more freedom. At the very least, everyone I knew had too much junk in the basement and too many e-mails. Those who were lucky enough to keep their jobs through the recession often worked longer hours than they liked to pay for stuff they were not sure they needed. Many of us yearned for a different way of living and a sense that our lives mattered. When I confided to friends that I felt I wasn't fully using my gifts—that I was meant to be more than I had become so far—many sighed in recognition. Their lives had not turned out as they had expected either.

I couldn't help thinking of my own mother, a high school graduate who worked for forty-three years but never had a job that fully utilized her sharp mind. At eighty-two, as lung disease sapped her strength, she came to our redbrick home for Easter dinner. At the end of the evening, I walked her out to her gold Chevy Cavalier, mindful of her cautious steps and aware of a shared but unspoken intuition that this would be her last holiday at our home. She paused at the car door, turned to me, and said wistfully, "I guess if I hadn't had you, my life wouldn't have been worth anything."

I loved my children, but I never wanted to lay that kind of trip on them. It was too great a burden to be someone else's only purpose. I'd wanted to stay home to nurse my babies when they were little. I'd wanted to read to them and sled with them on snow days. I believed that nurturing other human beings was important, undervalued work, which I didn't want to undervalue myself just because it didn't count on my Social Security statements. I wanted to honor the work of parenting, but I didn't want to disappear in it, especially now that my children were becoming increasingly independent. More to the point, it was partly my love for my children that was motivating a deep, churning desire to prevent my generation from screwing up their futures irreparably.

At forty-nine, I began taking small steps toward a renewal I couldn't yet name. I went back through decades of journals, trying to pinpoint when and how I had lost touch with the pieces of myself that were struggling to resurface. I gave away half the stuff in the basement and sold our fossil fuel stock. I also joined a group of spiritually grounded activists who were working to stop mountaintop removal coal mining, a devastating practice that contributed to both global warming and high rates of cancer in Appalachia. At the group's monthly meetings, I started singing again, which felt symbolic of some deeper transformation that involved claiming my power and my gifts. Most importantly, I remembered I was not alone.

Being part of a group that was strategic and sang on key made me feel immensely better, bolstering my courage for a solitary journey back to southern Africa, where I celebrated my fiftieth birthday and learned how rain had become unpredictable and maize crops had diminished. As a descendant of Irish Potato Famine survivors, I couldn't ignore the link between global warming and famine. As a parent, I couldn't be apathetic about the future. And so, only thirteen months after my midlife despair hit, I stood in front of the wrought iron White House fence, calmly waiting to hear the police issue their first warning.

Forty-eight of us would be arrested that February day. In addition to the well-known names, there were ranchers from Texas and Nebraska struggling to protect their grazing land from the Keystone XL Pipeline, which was scheduled to pump the world's dirtiest oil from Alberta, Canada to the Gulf of Mexico to be refined for export. The pipeline was the headline issue at this action, but those in parallel struggles were participating, too. Cherri Foytlin, Louisiana mother of six, had walked over twelve hundred miles to Washington, DC almost three years earlier to demand action on the BP oil spill disaster that had contaminated thousands of miles of Gulf Coast. Maria Gunnoe had gotten death threats for standing up to the powerful coal companies that were literally blowing the tops off the mountains of her native West Virginia.

I was there representing Earth Quaker Action Team, the group that had taught me to ground my social activism in spirituality and song— the group that had helped me see that my personal renewal was linked to this wider movement and a rising tide of change. Two friends had come to support me and were standing nearby, while others back home held me in prayer.

It seemed fitting that I was committing civil disobedience for the first time on Ash Wednesday, the first of the forty-day season of Lent that precedes Easter. Twenty minutes before we walked across the street to the White House, Minister Jim Antal mounted the stage in Lafayette Square in a red baseball cap and a clerical collar to explain what committing civil disobedience on this holy day meant to him as a Christian.

"Ash Wednesday is a good day to be arrested," he told the crowd of supporters and reporters. "It's a day of conscience, repentance, and conviction; a day when we take stock of our personal lives—and our life together on the planet . . . a good day to realign our lives with God's desire to preserve this good creation." Then he offered ashes to Robert Kennedy, Jr. and others who wanted them and joined the rest of the forty-eight as we walked across the street alongside the press, their microphone booms bobbing overhead.

Growing up in an Irish Catholic family, I had thought Lent was about giving up candy or ice cream, so you could virtuously binge on jelly beans and chocolate bunnies Easter morning. Lent seemed to be about guilt and self-denial, so I'd rejected it when I left my family's faith. In recent years, though, I'd become more open-minded, especially because Lent was a special time of reflection and fasting for my Roman Catholic husband, Tom. Now at midlife, I heard Jim's words about conscience, repentance, and conviction as something hopeful—steps toward transformation. It was about taking stock of my own life and the society that had shaped it. Taking stock in order to make a change.

"This is your first warning," blared the megaphone after the reporters had moved behind a side barricade, leaving the line of uniformed police in plain view. I stood shoulder to shoulder with the others and smiled. I felt more aligned with my values than I had since living in an African village almost three decades earlier.

Chapter One:
Because of Other People

A person is a person because of other people.

—Tswana proverb

I joined the Peace Corps in 1984—the year Apple introduced the Macintosh personal computer and Daryl Hannah starred in *Splash* with Tom Hanks. A recent college grad from the Philadelphia suburbs, I was assigned to teach for two and a half years in Bobonong, a village poised on the eastern tip of Botswana between South Africa and Zimbabwe. When I arrived at my post for the first time in a rusty Ford pickup, the road was not yet paved, though wooden pegs along the edges of the dusty track indicated that tarmac was planned. It was taking a long time, my ride explained, because people kept lifting the wooden markers for firewood, the main cooking fuel in a region where the land was arid, and women walked miles to gather branches from thorny acacia trees.

Along the road, I saw women carrying implausible loads—a heap of firewood or a sack of ground maize balanced on top of colorful head scarves—while young boys herded bony donkeys or cattle. As the bumpy road entered the village, round huts of mud and dung appeared, topped with grass roofs. Sprinkled among these rondavels were small rectangular houses made of cinder block with sloping, corrugated tin roofs. I could feel my heart beat fast as I peered out the pickup window at thin streams of smoke rising above low mud walls that shielded small cooking fires.

After passing a small grocery store and a bar, we turned left and headed up an even bumpier road to the junior secondary school where I'd be teaching English along with Brian, another member of my Peace Corps training group. We were each assigned a tiny cinder block house with a tin roof and a small fenced yard. There was a spigot outside my green kitchen door, but no running water inside and no electricity. In one room, I had a small table for eating and grading papers, two wooden chairs, and a propane-fueled stove with two burners. The other room, which I had to walk outside to access, had a single metal bed frame, a mattress, and a family of sun spiders that scampered up and down the walls, their bodies the size of quarters with legs the length of matches.

I stepped outside and took a deep breath to bolster my courage before sweeping out the harmless but intimidating spiders. I surveyed two rows of rectangular teacher housing, a path to the communal pit latrines, and beyond them the school, an assortment of pink one-story buildings laid out in the shape of a U with a dusty yard in the middle. Behind my house I saw scattered rondavels and, in the distance, the rust-colored Lepokole Hills, known for their Stone Age cave paintings.

In addition to a backpack and a guitar, I had arrived in Bobonong with a bachelor's degree from Duke, a vague sense of idealism, and no teaching experience. My undergraduate major had been comparative area studies, which meant I'd taken classes like "Southeast Asian Music" and studied abroad twice, in Tunisia and Ireland. The few interviews I'd had at Duke's career counseling office had convinced me that I didn't want a job that required high heels, but other than that, I didn't have a clear sense of purpose. I'd loved camping with the Girl Scouts, and the Peace Corps seemed kind of like a long, exotic camping trip. In hindsight, I'm embarrassed to admit I wasn't more altruistic or discerning than that.

Aside from the contour of the Lepokole Hills in the distance, the most beautiful part of my village was the extravagant night sky. There were only a few privately owned generators and no streetlights, so there was little to detract from Orion or the Southern Cross, which seemed to hover just out of reach. I had never seen so many stars at once, the big constellations as well as a billion diamond specks, invisible back in the suburbs of Philadelphia, where I had grown up with a night sky that was never darker than watercolor grey. Although I had left my family's Roman Catholic church my freshman year of college when I realized that I didn't know what I believed, Bobonong's night sky made me feel connected to something greater than myself. After a few months, I stopped bothering with my flashlight and became attuned to the phases of the moon, which lit my way on the rocky village paths.

Brian was my first friend in Bobonong, an outdoorsy Arizonan with a reddish-brown mustache who had worked as a "Hot Shot," the elite crew that put out forest fires. We were both immediately invited to join the other expatriate teachers for afternoon tea at the home of a British man, who served Earl Grey and biscuits at four, no matter how hot it was in the relentless Botswana sun. The bar was one of the only places to get even a moderately chilled drink, so on weekends we headed there with the Peace Corps volunteers across the village for Lion or Castle beer, made in South Africa. Other evenings I pulled out my guitar and we started belting out songs, like Simon & Garfunkel's "Homeward Bound" or "Take It Easy" by the Eagles.

I had learned during Peace Corps training how to greet people with "*Dumela*," addressing women as "*mma*" and men as "*rra*" with a rolling R that stuck on my American tongue. I was comfortable being friendly to everyone, but I was unsure how to make real African friends, especially since I was the only female teacher in our school. In Tswana culture, inviting male colleagues over for dinner would appear suggestive in a way that it wasn't with Brian or the other Western volunteers, who expected to socialize with each other. Since I didn't want to only hang out with other Westerners, I was grateful to meet Mmadithapelo, a librarian at the village high school.

Tall and thin with a short Afro and a strong laugh, Mmadithapelo enjoyed hanging out with Americans, who appreciated her independence and outspokenness. She was a few years older than I was, which she said made her like a big sister, giving her an excuse to gently boss me around. After her first visit to my cinder block house for a cup of tea, she walked in her stilettos and calf-length A-line skirt to my wire gate and demanded, "*Mma*, aren't you going to *buledisa* me?"

"What does that mean?" I asked with a smile.

"You always walk your guest halfway home," she began, "no matter how far away they live. If I live in that house there," she said pointing to the teacher's house next door, "you walk me to the fence between the houses. If I live in a village ten kilometers away," she said pointing to the horizon, "you walk me five kilometers. That's how we Africans do it."

Mmadithapelo's house in the village was a twenty-minute walk on a rocky path, so I walked with her for ten, stopping halfway down the hill that led to the main road and the grocery store. Henceforth, we always *buledisaed* each other, often standing at the halfway point on the hill for an extra hour, talking about the differences between our cultures or laughing at some gossip about the teachers' love lives.

In the following months, Mmadithapelo taught me how to properly kill a chicken, holding its body firmly so that it didn't get up and run around headless while its nerves were still twitching. She plunged the carcass into scalding water to make the plucking easier and cooked every part, including the head and feet. She also showed me how to cook *morogo wa dinawa*, greens with peanut butter, one of the rare vegetable dishes in a cuisine dominated by carbohydrates, like *phaleche*, the thick corn meal that was a staple in southern Africa. I thought of *phaleche* as a cross between grits and mashed potatoes, but Mmadithapelo laughed at me when I added a few slabs of butter.

"That's not how we eat it," she explained.

Mmadithapelo also laughed as I learned how to carry a bucket of water on my head, a vital skill for any village woman. There were communal taps sprinkled throughout the village, usually surrounded by girls filling their buckets, or for the smallest girls, an old rectangular tin. The girls hoisted their containers onto their heads and then sauntered away with one arm gracefully reaching up to balance it. When I tried to imitate them, it was not so graceful. The water sloshed over the lid of the bucket as I tried to settle it on my crown, causing the girls to break into excited giggles. Somehow, they could laugh without spilling their water, but when I started laughing, too, my bucket only sloshed more.

"*Mma*, look how much water you are wasting!" admonished Mmadithapelo. By the time I got back to her compound, my shirt was usually soaked, as she shook her head in amused disapproval.

Mmadithapelo lived in one half of a two-room, white cinder block house with black trim around the windows. In the other half lived an immigration worker in her twenties named Mosetsana, her seven-year-old brother Mopati, and her baby girl Kefilwe. After several months of living in the teacher housing, I decided to rent the rondavel next door to them within the same wire-fenced yard. We all shared a wooden pit latrine several yards behind the houses and the outdoor kitchen area, where Mosetsana cooked *phaleche* in a small, three-legged iron caldron.

I loved the round walls and thatched roof of my hut, which was much cooler in summer than cinder block, especially when the door and three windows were open and air flowed in every direction. With my bed against one section of wall, a small table against another, and a shelf for my two-burner gas stove, I had everything I needed in what I later estimated was 180 square feet. When I needed more space than that, I simply stepped outside and joined Mmadithapelo on the wooden chairs in front of her house for a cup of tea or sat with Mosetsana by the fire. Mosetsana was shy about speaking English, so she often communicated with me through the wide, gap-toothed smiles that lit up her beautiful face, as I tried to learn her language, Setswana.

Most of my teaching colleagues preferred to converse in English rather than listen to me grope for words in their native language. I appreciated that Mmadithapelo, though fluent in English, was willing to help me improve my Setswana. I was fascinated by its distinctive grammatical structure, where the first few letters of a noun signify what kind of thing it is. So, for example, a Motswana is a person whose first language is Setswana, and the plural of Motswana is Batswana, while the country's name is Botswana.

The phrase "*Motho ke motho ka botho*" ("A person is a person because of other people") captured the sense of interconnection and reciprocity that was at the core of Tswana culture. People helped each other at planting and harvest time in an agricultural system where land use was allocated by the village chief, not privately owned. Mmadithapelo explained, "If I have a field and I want the weeds taken out, people will come and help." She said she would make some porridge or other food, and after the work everyone would sit and eat together. "You just relax and talk to each other," she said simply. "No one would expect to be paid."

In Setswana, there was no difference between "borrow" and "lend," unlike in English where each verb designated the item's original owner.

"Teacher, borrow me your pen," a student would say when their hand-me-down Bic ran out of ink.

As I handed over my pen, I tried to explain, for the hundredth time, that I was lending it, and they were borrowing it. The students had a hard time with this distinction because in Setswana sharing was reciprocal. In the village, if one neighbor owned an ax and another a wheelbarrow, they shared their tools, without marking who originally owned what. Borrowing and lending were literally foreign concepts.

If a woman was cooking dinner and realized she was out of onions, she asked her neighbor for an onion, instead of walking a mile in the scorching heat to the village store, as the white people did. I was taken aback by the frequency with which people asked to borrow things from me, but gradually I realized that I was meant to reciprocate. When I finally started asking my neighbors for onions or eggs, they were delighted. It put us in real relationship in a way we were not when I was always the benefactor. The reluctance of most white volunteers to ask for help was seen as a sign of their aloofness, their unwillingness to be real equals, though the Westerners assumed they were being good neighbors by keeping to themselves.

At first the fact that most people didn't say "please" or "may I" seemed rude to me until I started to understand the cultural assumptions around sharing. Since it was the norm for people to help each other, you could ask for what you needed without ceremony. In fact, the word closest in meaning to "please" in Setswana was more like begging and implied that the person being asked couldn't be trusted to be generous. What sounded polite to Western ears was actually a subtle sign of mistrust.

Our students exemplified the ethos of sharing. One weekend our school went to a sports meet in a distant village. Eighty students crammed into the back of a long, three-ton flatbed truck, while the teachers took turns riding in the cab. The cold winter wind and the lack of leg space would have been enough to spur the average American teenager into a tirade of complaints, but these village youth happily packed themselves in for the seven-hour journey, spreading their blankets like a giant patchwork quilt to keep warm. Despite numerous detours and delays, the young teenagers laughed and sang Setswana church songs with one girl calling out the first line and the rest responding in harmony.

I took my turn riding in the back of the truck with the students just as the sun started moving below the acacia trees that lined the road. One girl looked my way and shouted, "*Mistress o a sitwa!*" ("The mistress is cold!")

Every student in the vicinity immediately offered me a blanket, despite the fact that I was dressed warmly, and they were not.

The ethos of sharing was not always so comfortable for me, as a white Westerner. Everyone assumed I was wealthy, and in one sense I was. I had education, access to a Peace Corps doctor, and the knowledge that my government would take care of me if there were ever an emergency. I could apply to a US embassy fund to get grants for special school projects, which I did along with other Peace Corps volunteers. At the same time, I was living on a volunteer stipend, making considerably less money than my African colleagues, though they seemed to get hit up a lot less frequently.

Often when I walked in public, small children ran up to me yelling, "*Dumela lekgowa. Mpha madi!*" ("Hello white person. Give me money!") For the children, it was a funny game, but for each Peace Corps volunteer the endless requests posed a dilemma. I heard of one new trainee who gave to everyone who asked during a visit to a village and ended up needing a loan from another American to get back to the Peace Corps training site. Although I gave away the occasional coins, I was more likely to joke with the children and get them to giggle at my Setswana. Sometimes I bought a handmade basket sold by village women or a jar of the beautiful ringed agates that children collected along the Bobonong roads, even when I knew they were overcharging me.

One time my mother sent a care package of Girl Scout cookies— two whole boxes, Samoas and Thin Mints. After a moment's excitement, I realized a dilemma. If I opened the boxes at school, where I'd received the package, I would be immediately surrounded by hundreds of children with their hands out. None of them would get very much, I told myself. More importantly, *I* wouldn't get very much. And the kids wouldn't appreciate that these were Girl Scout cookies. Sure they'd like the sugar, but these cookies meant something special to me, a Girl

Scout for thirteen years. I'd even received a Girl Scout award for my exemplary community spirit. These cookies were for *me*.

I found Brian, who also had a sweet tooth, and pulled him into the school library, locking the door behind us. We sat on the floor in the corner, the one spot where we couldn't be seen from any of the windows.

"I used to sell these door-to-door in my neighborhood," I told him as we devoured the Thin Mints and Samoas, reminiscing about home, and feeling a bit naughty. We wiped the crumbs from around our lips before we unlocked the door.

Fortunately, none of our students were starving. Botswana, by the mid-1980s, was hailed as one of most prosperous and well-run countries in Africa, thanks to a combination of prudent leadership and the discovery of diamonds shortly after their independence from Great Britain in 1966. The government had put much of the diamond money into building schools, hospitals, and roads—infrastructure that was completely overlooked under British rule. Although Botswana had experienced several years of drought by the time I arrived, I saw none of the distended bellies my parents were seeing on television from famine-ridden Ethiopia, which in 1985 inspired the transatlantic, star-studded concert known as Live Aid.

Traditionally, Tswana culture included a number of practices that helped protect the least fortunate from hunger. Everyone was expected to help plow and tend a special field that belonged to the chief, who kept the extra harvest in good times, but was supposed to share it when there was need in the community. Another custom was *mafisa,* where a man who owned many cattle would lend one or two cows to a man whose herd was smaller, giving the poorer family access to regular milk and giving the cows access to diverse grazing areas. In a region with unreliable rain, *mafisa* protected livestock against drought and disease, the way mutual funds spread out the risk of owning stock.

During my time in Botswana in the 1980s, the old ways were breaking down, though sometimes they coexisted with new practices, as in the case of religion. Traditionally the Batswana believed in a remote supreme being, called *Modimo,* the word the Christian missionaries appropriated for God. In daily affairs, however, many traditional Batswana called on their ancestors, or *badimo,* who operated something like a communion of saints. The ancestors could help people in their daily lives or punish them when they got out of line. They could also act as intermediaries, appealing to *Modimo* for general blessings, like rain. When Brian started dating a woman from the village, he was shocked to find that she both attended church and slaughtered a goat to honor her ancestors.

Despite cultural changes, cattle were still the primary markers of wealth and status in the village. A Motswana saving for retirement would buy livestock, not corporate stock, so my students found it peculiar that a presumably wealthy white woman like myself came from a family that owned no cattle. Once, when we received a pile of letters from their American pen pals, I sat with some students in the library explaining unfamiliar vocabulary. One American girl had drawn a picture of a hamburger and fries, which our students had never heard of before. Another wrote that she had a gerbil and a rabbit, and inquired if her African pen pal had any pets. None of my students had ever heard the word gerbil, but as I tried to explain what it was and why a child might keep one in her house, I felt the cultural chasm opening between us.

Finally one of my brightest students turned to her companions and explained authoritatively, "They don't keep cattle. They only keep rabbits and rats." The surrounding girls exploded in laughter.

I often seemed to be a source of amusement. Occasionally a group of girls would huddle around my desk to ask for a pen or help with their English homework, when they really just wanted to touch my short, straight, brown hair. When I caught them, they giggled and covered their mouths shyly. Something about being white made everything I did potentially funny, especially when I broke their stereotypes of white people by speaking more than a few words of Setswana.

One school vacation, I decided to spend a week with the women and children of the Tidimane family, who had given me the nickname Nchadi (which means "dear one"). The women spoke less English than Mmadithapelo, so I figured a week at their farm would improve my Setswana. It did, but it was mentally exhausting. I found myself volunteering for manual labor just to escape the constant effort of sitting around chatting. One chore I found surprisingly enjoyable was coating the floor of an old rondavel with a new layer of mud and dung. I dipped a rag in the bucket of earthy-smelling muck and swept it in a circular motion, backing my knees slowly across the floor toward the door as I progressed, filling in the cracks and making it look like new.

The Tidimanes were amused that a white American would enjoy this messy job, so when they unexpectedly took me to stay with some relatives midweek, they boasted to our hosts that I had learned how to coat the floors.

"Don't they do that in America?" asked the matriarch in Setswana, as we sat around a fire on wooden stools.

"Oh, no," said Mrs. Tidimane, turning to me knowingly. "You don't do that in America, do you?"

I had been struggling to keep up with the conversation, and now that the spotlight was on me, my mind went blank. My Setswana grammar was very good—Mmadithapelo claimed that I could write the language better than she could—but without a dictionary in hand my vocabulary was limited, especially when the conversation moved beyond everyday pleasantries. Sitting in a compound of remote rondavels—with nothing beyond the mud walls but bush and the distant sound of singing in the night—how could I possibly explain that I had grown up in a suburban apartment where the floors were linoleum, wood, and tile? I wracked my brain for relevant vocabulary to explain how different my home was.

"We do not spread dung in America," I said feebly in Setswana. "We have no dung because we have no cows."

After a moment of silence, the five adults around me burst into guffaws that lasted a full ten minutes, the matriarch's breasts heaving. The white-haired man next to her looked like he might fall off his wooden folding chair. I laughed, too, though a little self-consciously, uncertain what was funny: the fact that a white American was talking about cow dung in Setswana or the fact that my family was too poor to own any cattle.

For the next two days, more and more people filled the compound, a cluster of rondavels encircled by a low mud wall. I eventually figured out they were celebrating the engagement of a daughter and the ritual giving of blankets from the groom's family to the bride's. In a few months, this would be followed by cattle, an exchange meant to cement the relationship, not just between two individuals, but between the two families. Between plates of beef and *phaleche*, whenever there was a lull in conversation, the white-haired old man would say, "We have no dung because we have no cows!" and the circle would burst into laughter again.

The moments when I could glimpse my own culture through Batswana eyes were always instructive. Sometimes people would ask me if it was true that people in the United States put their elders in institutions, incomprehensible in a country where grandparents were a revered and integral part of the family. Often my students called me "fat and beautiful" as a compliment, though I couldn't help wincing. I had put on fifteen pounds since adding *phaleche* to my daily diet—not to mention milk that came with the cream still on top—but in my culture fat was a sign of gluttony. In Botswana it was a sign of food security.

There were constant reminders of how much more Americans consumed of everything from furniture to food. One day I tried to explain to my English class what a doorbell was, but none of the kids could conceive of a house so big that simply calling out *"koko"* ("knock, knock") at the gate wouldn't do. For Easter, my mother sent me a care package, and I opened it in front of a Motswana colleague, who had stopped by for a visit. I offered him some jelly beans, but struggled to explain why my mother had included a bag of pink and green plastic grass, not to mention a pink plastic basket. Botswana was famous for its beautifully woven grass baskets, whose circular patterns looked surprisingly like the traditional Hopi ones I had seen in museums at home. My pink plastic basket looked tacky in comparison.

I missed only a few things from the United States—mint chocolate chip ice cream, Hellmann's mayonnaise, and a few close friends, whose letters I treasured. I didn't miss television or malls. I didn't mind not having a car or a phone. I didn't miss mirrors or shaving my legs. I didn't even mind the pit latrines or having to heat my water to bathe in a basin. I certainly didn't miss news stories about crime and the crack epidemic that was ravaging American cities or the restless ambition of most students at Duke. The slow pace of village life seemed much saner.

In Bobonong, there was always time for a cup of tea, a song, or to *buledisa* your guest. Crime was rare and teachers were respected, so I walked alone at night and hitchhiked without fear. Being able to borrow things meant I didn't need to own much. Being able to watch the Southern Cross traverse the night sky was entertainment enough. At the end of my first year, I wrote in my journal, "I think I might be content being poor for the rest of my life."

Twenty-seven years later, when I reread my journals in the office of my new five-bedroom house in Philadelphia, that sentiment felt painfully naive, though the idea that my humanity was rooted in my connection to other people felt truer than ever.

Chapter Two:
Things Fall Apart

Things fall apart; the center cannot hold;
Mere anarchy is loosed upon the world.
—William Butler Yeats

Although I loved living simply in a village, I eventually realized that simplicity was not the same as poverty. Witnessing the effects of colonialism as I traveled around the region during school vacations woke me up to the plight of the truly poor and planted the idea that things only changed when people struggled to change them. In some ways, it was what I learned in neighboring South Africa and Zimbabwe that led me to handcuff myself to the White House fence a few decades later, though at the time I was living in southern Africa it was impossible to imagine that those dispossessed by colonialism would have that injustice compounded by global warming, which I wouldn't even hear about for another few years.

For most of my two and a half years in the Peace Corps, I taught English, but one term I was asked to teach southern African history to cover for a teacher who had just left. Although I knew little of the material that would be on the students' national exams, I found a few books and started studying. The hardest part was figuring out how to pronounce the Zulu names, like Senzangakhona, King Shaka's father, and Dingiswayo, Shaka's mentor. I spent the first few weeks trying not to humiliate myself in front of my class of forty fidgety teenagers, cramming before each lesson like it was a college exam.

Most of the curriculum consisted of memorizing the names and birthdays of famous Africans. The textbook made any deeper understanding impossible since each chapter focused on a separate ethnic group, and was written by a different historian. One chapter gave a sanitized description of the bloody nineteenth-century British battles with the Zulu, another the Tsonga conflicts with the Portuguese, and another the Sotho alliance with the British that led to the creation of Lesotho, a little donut hole of a country surrounded by South Africa. There was a chapter on the conflict between the British and the Afrikaners—a group descended mostly from the Dutch—and another on the Germans and the Herero, the southwest African group whom the Germans tried to exterminate. Nowhere did it explain how these conflicts were related or why so many Europeans were in Africa to begin with.

One day in class—when I started to feel slightly more confident—I posed this question to my students and got forty blank stares. Turned out none of them knew what a European was. "The white people," I explained. "Which of these groups have white skin like me?"

"The Zulu," offered one boy confidently. Another student said the British were black. I glanced around the dim classroom, but no one was laughing.

I stood before a dusty chalkboard in my favorite African skirt, made of the blue-and-white finely patterned fabric of the Herero, who had adopted nineteenth-century German fashions and Africanized them in defiance. My skirt, the language we were speaking, the chalkboard behind me—our classroom was filled with the evidence of colonialism, but like many Americans, none of my village students knew that history. I took a deep breath, picked up a scrap of chalk, and made two lists on the grey slate, one of the Africans and one of the Europeans mentioned in their book. Then I began explaining colonialism in simple terms: "A long time ago, people from Europe came to Africa and fought Africans to take their land and the valuable stuff under their land, like diamonds and gold. . . ."

In a way, this was the part of my Peace Corps job for which I was best prepared. Growing up, I had heard about colonialism from my mother, the youngest child of Irish immigrants. Her five record albums included Irish nationalist songs like "A Nation Once Again" and "Four Green Fields," a metaphor for the four provinces of Ireland. The lyrics told the story of a "proud old woman" whose sons and grandsons fought to reclaim the land that "strangers" had taken from her. My mother explained how the English had stolen Irish land and beaten Irish school children for speaking their own language. Her greatest grievance was the Potato Famine that began in 1845. She told me how the English had exported meat and dairy from Ireland while at least a million peasants starved. Over a century later, my mother didn't like me listening to the Beatles because they were English.

When I studied in Dublin for a semester my junior year of college, I learned that at the time of the famine (which the Irish call *an Gorta Mór* or the Great Hunger), landlords, mostly of English descent, charged rent to a growing population of Irish peasants, who had become overly dependent on cheap potatoes. When the potato crop failed a few years in a row, some landlords offered their tenants modest food aid, but many used the opportunity to get rid of the peasants, who were more rebellious and less lucrative than livestock. Some landlords offered boat passage to cities like New York or Philadelphia. Others just evicted those who were behind on their rent, sending bailiffs to level their cottages in front of the starving family, burning the thatch and scattering the stones. The green fields of Ireland became dotted with docile sheep and commemorated in sentimental songs.

On my father's side, at least one of my great-grandmothers left Ireland as a teenager during the Hunger, presumably traveling on what the Irish called "coffin ships" because so many of their passengers died of typhoid. My father's family had settled in the anthracite-rich region of Pennsylvania, in the traditional territory of the Susquehannock Native Americans, where my great-grandfathers mined the coal that fueled US expansion. My mother's parents came to Philadelphia two generations later, in the early twentieth century, searching for economic opportunity in an American city—just as countless southern Africans had headed for Johannesburg after being forced out of their villages.

I saw many similarities between Ireland and southern Africa, and not just the remnants of British influence—cars on the left side of the road, Marmite yeast extract, and a ubiquitous addiction to tea. It wasn't only the grass roofs and the culture of singing either. The Irish proverb, "*I scath a chéile a mhaireann na daoine,*" (translated literally as, "People live in each other's shadows,") implied the same sense of interconnection as the Tswana saying, "A person is a person because of other people." I thought it fitting that *Things Fall Apart*, Africa's most famous novel about the disintegration caused by colonialism, took its title from an Irish poem written at the end of World War I as Ireland broke into open rebellion against the British.

As I stood in front of forty students in my crowded Bobonong classroom trying to explain colonialism in a colonial language, I was uncomfortably aware of my own odd spot in history. "My ancestors were conquered by the British, too!" I threw in at one point to show my solidarity, but that just confused matters. Ireland may have been England's first overseas conquest, but in southern Africa, the dividing lines had been black and white. I may have sympathized with the conquered, but I looked like the conquerors.

Botswana's colonial history was less severe than Ireland's partly because its fields weren't as green. In fact, much of the landlocked country was taken up by the Kalahari Desert. Aside from a little gold near Francistown, the British thought the Batswana didn't possess much worth having other than a route between its more desirable colonies. Although it became a protectorate in the British colonial system in 1885, local chiefs continued to do much of the day-to-day governing, and the dry land stayed mostly in African control. In hindsight, Botswana was lucky that its Orapa diamonds were not discovered until 1967, a full century after South Africa's gems.

In the more verdant and strategically situated South Africa, it was a different story. In 1652, the Dutch East India Company established an outpost on the southwestern tip of Africa to supply its fleet of ships on their long journey between Amsterdam and Asia, where they acquired Indonesian spices, Chinese silk, and Japanese silver. Often described as the first multinational corporation, it had its own military and was the first company to publicly sell stock. Over the next century, the Khoikhoi and San, the indigenous residents of what became Cape Town, were killed, expelled, enslaved, or infected with European diseases like smallpox. Over the following centuries, Europeans expanded north and east, battling Africans and each other for the territory and vast mineral wealth below.

By the beginning of the twentieth century, Europeans owned most South African land, though most of the population remained African—Zulu, Xhosa, Sotho, Tswana, Pedi, and Venda, among others. With their remaining territory crowded and overgrazed, and exorbitant taxes imposed by the colonial government, many Africans were driven from their villages to work in the mines or the growing cities, where there were also significant numbers of mixed race people and those whose ancestors had come to South Africa as indentured servants from India. By the mid-twentieth century, whites had formalized the political system known as apartheid, which literally meant "separation" or "apartness" for the races, restricting where people could live, whom they could marry, and whether they could vote. Whole communities were removed by bulldozer because they were deemed to be in the wrong place.

From the beginning, Africans resisted: singing songs that told their version of history and taking to the streets—sometimes nonviolently and sometimes with arms. In 1976, black students mobilized to protest an unjust education system, worsened by the government's decision to make all subjects taught in Afrikaans, a language mostly derived from Dutch. At least 176 students were killed in the ensuing uprising. By the mid-1980s, when I was in the Peace Corps, the poor, urban townships were in constant revolt, as the white government resorted to increasingly murderous repression, which only fueled the resistance. Televised images of youth throwing stones and being met with bullets fanned the movement for US universities and cities to divest from companies doing business in South Africa.

Some South Africans went into exile, including the deputy headmaster of our school, Sam Rahube, who had brought his family to Botswana after serving ten years on Robben Island, the notoriously brutal prison where Nelson Mandela was held. Mr. Rahube had a calm strength and a commitment to our students that everyone respected. Despite growing up in a viciously racist system, he was the African teacher who spent the most time mentoring the waves of inexperienced white foreigners sent to teach in Bobonong. Mr. Rahube was one of the few people who seemed equally comfortable with people from

Botswana, Lesotho, Canada, Denmark, the United Kingdom, and the United States. He was too much of a gentleman to point out that I was unqualified to teach his country's history.

Many black South Africans living in Botswana frowned upon Peace Corps volunteers who traveled in South Africa as tourists. The mostly white volunteers would say they wanted to see apartheid for themselves, but without a local guide in a country whose black areas were wracked by violence, they ended up posing for photographs on the "whites only" benches and eating lobster in Durban. Not wanting to emulate them, I had decided not to vacation in South Africa, though I did travel through it one Christmas en route to the small mountain kingdom of Lesotho. Almost accidentally, the other volunteer I was traveling with and I connected with locals who helped us to see South Africa's extremes of wealth and poverty during our brief transit.

Johannesburg in the 1980s reminded me of Philadelphia, with wide highways, sprawling malls, video games, pools, and all the other marks of affluence that I didn't miss. I felt strangely uncomfortable, partly because I knew about the repressive political system that had created white wealth and partly because it felt so much like the United States at Christmas with its emphasis on frantic shopping. The trains ran on time, the telephones worked—things that Botswana couldn't yet claim—but after one night in a white woman's large Johannesburg home, I felt relieved to arrive in Lesotho where we spent Christmas in a missionary-owned rondavel in a remote mountain village.

On our way back through South Africa, we met an Irish priest in his fifties who dropped everything to show us the poor, rural region that he served. We saw rows of tiny, identical redbrick houses built by the government of Bophuthatswana, one of the patchwork "homelands" created by the apartheid government to mask the disenfranchisement of its black citizens and separate them by ethnic group.

"Now we're in South Africa," he said as we drove across some invisible line on the barren landscape. "Now we're in Bophuthatswana," he said a few minutes later as we crossed another invisible line. This happened several times, illustrating the absurdity of the supposed border.

The priest also took us to a desolate area where he said that women and children had been left to scrape by while men sought work in the mines or factories in town. Malnutrition was high, with little or no medical care available. He explained in a familiar brogue that the government had moved people here, assigned them to plots, and then put up a few pit latrines. The resourceful women had thrown together whatever kind of homes they could, mostly out of scrap metal that was burning hot in summer and cold in winter. Most homes had magazines for wallpaper and stones on top of the corrugated tin to keep the roofs from blowing away. I tried to surreptitiously snap photos from a discrete distance as shockingly thin children waved to us from the road.

Seeing apartheid in person helped me understand a peculiar aspect of Setswana, which was also spoken in parts of South Africa. While most words for people started with "mo-" like Motswana, the word for white person, *lekgowa*, started with "le-," putting it in the same noun class as "drunk," "thief," "prostitute," and "fool." While I felt awkward about this association, I understood why whites were viewed as "other." It was the same resentment that made my mother dislike the Beatles. In South Africa in the 1980s, the forced removals weren't even over yet, the bulldozers reminding me of the sheriffs who dismantled Irish cottages and scattered their residents during the Great Hunger just so someone else could claim the land.

Resentment was still palpable in neighboring Zimbabwe, where the long, bitter struggle to end white minority rule had ended only a few years before I joined the Peace Corps. In Botswana when I was the only white person on a bus, I received either smiles or indifference from my fellow passengers. In Zimbabwe, I received scorching glares when I boarded a bus and carried my backpack down the crowded aisle to a seat near the rear.

Despite the history of racial tension, Zimbabwe was a popular country for Peace Corps volunteers to vacation during school breaks. Harare was larger and more modern than Botswana's capital—with the latest Sylvester Stallone flick in theatres and Madonna's "Into the Groove" on the radio. There were elegant, modern hotels, but also uniquely African attractions, like game parks with zebra and rhino, and the ancient stone ruins of Great Zimbabwe, evidence of a civilization that far predated British rule. During one vacation, Maureen, my best friend from Duke, flew into Harare, and we hitchhiked to the breathtaking falls known as Mosi-oa-Tunya before the explorer David Livingstone renamed them after Queen Victoria. Maureen posed laughing next to a sign warning of crocodiles, with the white mist of Victoria Falls behind her.

Back in Bobonong—which Maureen visited briefly before flying home—I tried to support the new country by buying butter from Zimbabwe rather than South Africa, but the truth was that in the mid-eighties most of the productive land was still owned by the descendants of white settlers, and the question of land reform was thorny. The country had a black ruler, Robert Mugabe, but the fierceness and determination that had made him a successful liberation leader were now making him intolerant of political dissent, and there were rumors of violence between the two major African political parties.

Once, I visited a farm near Bobonong and discovered a family of Zimbabwean refugees quietly living with my Batswana friends. One night, as we sat around the fire, the Zimbabwean patriarch expressed his surprise that a white woman would come way out to the country to sleep on an African mud floor.

"Isn't she afraid that you might slit her throat in the night?" he asked seriously in Ndebele, and all the Batswana laughed heartily before translating his question for me.

No, it had never occurred to me that someone might slit my throat. Not in peaceful Botswana—though it was increasingly affected by the violence of the surrounding region.

In 1985, my second year in the Peace Corps, the South African government conducted the first of two "raids" into Botswana, claiming to be hunting terrorists. In the middle of the night, nearly fifty white soldiers crossed the border and massacred twelve people in the capital, Gaborone. Some of the dead were South Africans living in exile in Botswana. A few were Batswana. After the second such raid, the Botswana military—which I hadn't even known existed before—suddenly had a public presence, trying to look like it was doing something useful in the face of white South Africa's overwhelming military might.

One day soon afterwards, I was riding the bus from Gaborone back toward Bobonong when we were flagged down and boarded by Batswana soldiers at a roadblock. Again the only white person, I was asked to exit and dump the contents of my bag on the dusty ground, so a soldier could casually inspect my underwear and toiletries, his gun slung loosely over his shoulder. Presumably the soldiers had been told to look out for white South Africans, though it was obvious to the women on the bus that the strongest military in the region would not send the likes of me as their advance guard. My fellow passengers came to my defense, yelling out the bus windows for the soldiers to leave me alone. The soldier motioned for me to get back on the bus, where I was met with pats and nods of reassurance from the women.

I always felt safe with Batswana women, particularly the middle-aged village mothers. Once I took a train north from Gaborone on the last night of the month, the time when many Batswana got paid, so "*tsotsis*" ("thugs") were out stalking travelers. I had been to the bank myself and kept the bulk of my cash wadded up in the bottom of my suede boot with only enough for the train fare in my pocket. As soon as I paid for my ticket at an outdoor booth, an African man advanced toward me with the kind of smile that was too wide to feel friendly.

"Madame," he began solicitously in English. "You don't want to wait *here* with all these people. It's not safe. You can wait in first class." He pointed down the platform to the empty and dimly lit waiting room with benches but no witnesses. "I can escort you," he offered with a slight bow.

"*Nna rra*," I politely declined in Setswana so he'd know I wasn't some fresh-off-the-plane white woman with no sense.

I walked past him to a group of middle-aged women who were laying out their parcels on the platform. They looked strong, with thick middles and colorful headscarves and skirts. I greeted them in Setswana, shaking hands with my left palm on top of my right wrist, body language that showed respect. I asked them how they had gotten up that morning. They reciprocated, smiling that I understood Tswana custom. With their encouragement, I plopped myself among them on the train platform. When the loudspeaker announced that the train would be two hours late, we all stretched out, and I slept soundly with my head on my overnight bag, confident that no one would rob me as long as I was surrounded by these formidable village mothers. I felt sorry for anyone who thought they were safer alone in first class.

Traveling between the capital and the village, I could see that Botswana was changing. I could walk around Bobonong alone any time of the day or night, but people said to be careful in the city. A fellow volunteer was pickpocketed. Another had her apartment broken into, something I couldn't imagine in my village. Along with the urban population, violence, crime, and materialism were growing. Even without knowing about global warming—which was silently being fueled by industrialization around the world—I sensed there was a hidden cost to modernization.

"Development" meant becoming Westernized: eating processed hamburgers instead of freshly butchered beef; building hot, cinder block houses instead of cool, mud rondavels. It meant watching Hollywood movies and trying to catch up to the West technologically. Gaborone got its first traffic light while I was there, which they called a "robot." Then it got a pizza joint. The changes sounded fantastic to people from the village. Once when some of our students went to Gaborone for a sports meet, the math teacher brought them as a special treat to a clothing store with a short escalator. They spent an hour riding it up and down, shrieking.

While Bobonong celebrated Botswana's twentieth anniversary of independence with singing, traditional dancing, and a donkey race, Gaborone had fireworks, which Mmadithapelo described as "exploding colored stars" since it was one of the rare English words she didn't know. During my last months in Bobonong, Mmadithapelo moved to Gaborone to take a library course at the university, but she didn't like city life. One day, she scolded the men she shared a cab with for not saying hello and inquiring how she had gotten up.

"Are we not Africans?" she asked indignantly, and they contritely issued the required Setswana greetings, which were ubiquitous in the village.

Such anecdotes made me ambivalent about teaching English, even though I knew our students needed it to get a job or to read seed packages if they became farmers. Not much was published in Setswana, so learning English opened them to the world, which South African students had fought for in 1976 when the apartheid government tried to make them learn in the Dutch-derived Afrikaans. English enabled my students in Bobonong to read simplified versions of *The Adventures of Tom Sawyer* and *Things Fall Apart*. Still, I wasn't convinced that teaching African kids the difference between "borrow" and "lend" was making the world a better place in the big scheme of things.

In several letters home I speculated that I might want to pursue development as a career, though I was suspicious of the economic policies promoted by the World Bank and the International Monetary Fund. The basic cause of poverty in southern Africa was that Europeans had seized the most fertile land and then forced Africans into mining or industrial jobs that were poorly paid. Nothing I could do would undo that injustice.

Part of what was confusing about the concept of development was that the positive and negative changes in Botswana seemed to go hand in hand. As the phone lines improved, personal communication broke down. Paved roads brought street violence. On the other hand, Mmadithapelo pointed out that she now had the right to choose her own husband, something her father would have done in an earlier era. I knew it was important for me not to romanticize traditional village life. As an outsider, I had experienced the best of a culture that could be oppressive to those who deviated from its norms, especially its gender norms. Many Batswana understandably yearned for the freedom and perks of my culture, as well as the material comforts.

During my last months in Bobonong, the road to town finally started taking shape. The bumpy dirt had been gradually leveled and graded, though I never saw anyone working on it. Then suddenly, a black carpet magically unrolled from the town, gradually moving toward the village. On the day I left, I hitched a ride in the back of a pickup truck, sitting on my backpack as the thatched roofs disappeared in the dust kicked up behind me. My eyes were filled with tears until I hit the tarmac that would lead me to the nearest town, then on to the capital, a little vacation travel, and an airplane ride home. The Bobonong road would be finished within weeks. I left with a sense that the village would never be the same and that neither would I.

Chapter Three:
In Each Other's Shadows

People live in each other's shadows.
—Irish proverb

I moved back to the United States in early 1987. Oprah Winfrey's show had recently become nationally syndicated, "Walk Like an Egyptian" was top of the pop charts, and Apple was about to release the first Macintosh to display color. In the two and half years I'd been gone, ATMs had replaced lines at the bank, as well as some of the bank tellers. A computer was replacing the card catalog at our local library. I felt as out of date as the typewriter I'd used at college, which now sat in the hall closet of my parents' apartment, along with the grass baskets I'd brought home from Botswana.

I'd grown up on the Main Line, the wealthy string of suburbs named after the Pennsylvania Railroad line that used to run from Philadelphia west toward Lancaster and on to Chicago. In the nineteenth century, some of Philadelphia's most prestigious families had built summer estates on land that had been the traditional territory of the Lenni-Lenape. In the early twentieth century, my immigrant grandparents—a maid and a blacksmith—had saved enough to move from West Philadelphia to Bala Cynwyd, on the Main Line's northeastern edge. My mother lived with them well into her thirties, commuting to a downtown office where she and her sister pushed paper punched cards into IBM computers the size of closets.

After both her parents died, my mother moved a few blocks away to a one-bedroom apartment over a storefront that flanked the Bala Theatre, whose tan stone facade sported a frescoed chariot and hieroglyphics from its silent film days as the Egyptian Theatre. When she married my father in 1960, he moved in with her. They invested her $4,000 inheritance in a laundromat at just the moment in US history when middle-class Americans were buying their own washing machines. A former workman on an oil tanker, my dad kept the books while mom did the wash, so it took her over a year to figure out how badly the business was doing. They declared bankruptcy when I was a baby and never left the one-bedroom apartment over the movie theatre where I grew up.

My mother was a changed woman after the bankruptcy, tighter with her finances and her trust—bankrupt of affection for my father, whom she blamed for the loss. While he became a bartender, she figured out how to keep their expenses less than their modest income, walking a mile to avoid putting a nickel in a parking meter and paying for everything with cash to avoid interest. She learned which thrift stores took clothes on consignment when we were done with them and which denominations had the best rummage sales (Jews and Episcopalians, she asserted). I don't recall her ever buying herself a new dress until my wedding, and that was the dress in which she was eventually buried.

Pantyhose were one of the few clothing items she bought new, though when she got a run, she cut off the damaged leg, kept it for dusting, and saved the rest of the pantyhose in her bottom drawer. When she'd done the same with a second pair, she'd wear the remaining good legs, two layers around her waist. She was an accidental environmentalist, discarding the little she threw away in leftover shopping bags because she considered buying trash bags a waste.

As a child, I didn't think of our lifestyle as simple or anything noble. A kid on financial aid at an elite private school, I wore secondhand clothes and hoped no one would recognize them. I thought of our one-bedroom apartment as an embarrassment, a reason to play at other children's houses, a reason to choose a college eight hours away. Coming home after the Peace Corps, I realized that our apartment had only seemed lacking compared to the large stone houses down the street. In Bobonong I'd never felt deprived because what I had was the norm.

After living in southern Africa, for the first time in my life I didn't feel ashamed of my working class Irish roots. Instead, I felt conflicted about the wealth and consumption around me.

To pass the months before I began a master's in African studies at Yale, I worked for caterers on the Main Line, where a wedding reception easily ran $30,000, well over the US national average annual income. Whether in an elegant private home or a chandelier-lit rented hall, there was a table during the appetizer hour stacked with bread, fruit, and cheese—a cornucopia arranged into a work of art but barely touched as we passed trays of fried wontons and chicken satay before the real meal even began. For a buffet, we cooked massive amounts of each dish, just in case everyone picked salmon one night instead of beef. Afterwards we packed a sample of leftovers for the hosts and dumped the rest into construction-strength trash bags.

A few years earlier, when I was at Duke, I might have wondered if I would have such an elegant wedding myself someday. Now, as I dumped aluminum trays full of prime filet and grilled chicken that had never been touched, I couldn't help but remember how Mmadithapelo had taught me not to waste even the chicken's feet or head. Other former volunteers were the only people who understood how alienated I felt. Brian, who had gone back to his home in Arizona, told me about walking into an American supermarket when he got back. After years of craving chocolate chip cookies, he'd stood under bright lights in the cookie aisle overwhelmed by the number of choices and finally left without buying anything.

Although the shop nearest my hut in Bobonong didn't have as much variety as one aisle of a US supermarket, I'd had something even better there—a relationship with the owner, James Mafokate. Once James discovered that I loved Cadbury bars, he'd kept me supplied with a daily dose of milk chocolate, which I washed down with a pint of fresh milk, a thin lip of cream on top. Granted, upon our reunion my mother had asked if I was pregnant, but there was something satisfyingly simple about knowing what my snack would be each afternoon on my way home from school and having the people who sold it to me greet me by name.

I had never paid much attention to my appearance—even less in

Bobonong since there were no mirrors. Suddenly I was back in a culture where mirrors were everywhere and "fat" was not a compliment. I joined the YMCA—an Olympic-length pool being a luxury unavailable in Bobonong—and swam off the fifteen pounds of Peace Corps weight gain, remaining in the middle of the "healthy" column on the weight charts until after my second child was born thirteen years later. When I visited Maureen—the college friend who had visited me in southern Africa—she gently mentioned that people in the United States still wore deodorant, a habit I had given up, along with shaving and wearing makeup. After Maureen's comment, I bought some deodorant, chagrined, but kept my hairy legs in defiance.

Feeling different from people I loved was the most painful part of coming home. When my father was in the hospital with a chronic mix of heart and lung problems, I visited him each day but didn't know what to talk about. I chatted more easily with Denise, another college friend, until she left the kitchen faucet running and felt criticized when I walked over and turned it off. I wanted to explain how hauling buckets on my head had taught me not to waste water, how little was actually needed to bathe when you used a shallow basin. I wanted to tell her about a woman I knew in Bobonong who wouldn't pour out the remnants of a cup of tea without walking it over to the nearest tree, but I struggled to figure out how to tell these stories without sounding like the kind of preachy zealot I had recoiled from in college.

I remembered one night five years earlier when I was a student at Duke. I was standing in the checkout line of the student snack bar, buying Mint Milano cookies for Maureen's stressed-out roommate, Patsy, and feeling pretty good about myself when I ran into a classmate who seemed to be majoring in student activism. She spotted the cookies and said, "Don't you care about tomato pickers?" Apparently Campbell's wasn't treating its farm workers right, and Campbell's owned Pepperidge Farm, which made the Mint Milanos.

"There is a boycott," she told me acidly, as if I should have known.

I left the encounter feeling defensive, muttering to myself that the woman would have been more effective if she hadn't tried to guilt trip me.

By the time I got home from the Peace Corps five years later, I felt like that anti-cookie woman—self-righteous and a bit insufferable. I went to a Bob Dylan/Grateful Dead concert and bought bumper stickers that said, "Stop Apartheid/Boycott Shell" and "Live Simply So Others May Simply Live." Unfortunately I was finding it difficult to live simply myself in the United States. While I could walk to work or the store in Bobonong, on the Main Line distances were farther, public transportation limited, and hitchhiking eccentric at best, so I used part of my Peace Corps readjustment allowance to buy a used Honda Civic to go with my "Live Simply" bumper sticker.

In graduate school, I started learning about the forces that undermined simple living. One of my first papers for the two-year program was about the colonization of the southern Batswana, those whose land became part of South Africa rather than Botswana. Before colonialism, I learned, men hunted game and tended cattle, while women collected wild food, like roots, and cultivated modest fields of sorghum. Because women traditionally went to live with their husbands' families, sisters were spread out geographically, making it more likely that at least one would get a decent crop in a region where rainfall was patchy at best. To increase everyone's food security, women brought their harvest to their mother, who distributed it to her daughters, keeping the best grain for the next year's seeds.

When English missionaries arrived among the southern Batswana in the early nineteenth century, they introduced the plow and the concept of individualism, along with the Bible. Operated by men, the plow increased crop yields, but it also undermined the old matrilineal system of sharing the harvest. Those who could afford the tool now had a big advantage over those who couldn't, especially after the discovery of diamonds and gold in South Africa created an explosion of demand for food in the emergent towns. Those with surplus maize—also introduced by the missionaries—could now sell it, instead of sharing it. Meanwhile, the amount of land with wild game and roots was steadily decreasing, taking away another source of food for those who had less to begin with.

Although I found such nineteenth-century history intriguing and enjoyed writing papers, I realized by my second year that I was primarily interested in history for the light it shed on current debates. At Yale, some professors and students argued that capitalism and the greed it encouraged were the root causes of apartheid, while others argued that in the late twentieth century, the self-interest of companies like Ford and Shell (who wanted educated workers) could be a liberalizing force in South Africa. I sympathized with the campus divestment movement, which had erected a tin shack outside the rare-books library to protest university investment in companies operating in South Africa. Strong economic pressure, they argued, was more likely to end apartheid than gradual, self-interested reform.

While my classes taught me abstract theories, I learned more about the human cost of apartheid from South Africans, like my friend, Kumi Naidoo, who had left his home in Durban when he found out he was due to be arrested under a state-of-emergency order that allowed for torture. His best friend had been brutally murdered by the regime, and now his brother was in prison. As an activist, he could not go home himself without risking a similar fate, yet he often found the relative comfort of living in the United States alienating. When the Yale Southern African Research Program hosted its biannual gathering, we were both horrified at the level of food waste at a sit-down dinner where each participant was served an entire Cornish game hen.

Finding friends who shared my values, I gradually realized, was the best antidote to feeling alienated, and a key to living simply. My four grad school housemates and I took turns cooking dinner, saving us all time and money. In Bobonong I had inherited furniture from former volunteers and passed it on when I left. The same worked in New Haven. Though I picked up a futon, a desk, and some bookshelves at IKEA, our house came with everything else—a dining room table, couch, vacuum, dishes, pots, pans, and the *Moosewood Cookbook*. I continued living in group houses through my twenties, learning to compost my banana peels and use canvas shopping bags from my more environmentally conscious housemates.

I still looked forward to blue airmail letters from Botswana with a picture of a baobab tree or a wild hare on the stamp. Mmadithapelo confirmed that the paved Bobonong road had brought more traffic. James Mafokate, the grocery store owner, wrote about the rain and how the maize was growing. Mr. Tidimane, whose family had hosted me at their farm, wrote entirely in Setswana, which became increasingly hard to remember. Sometimes I sat alone in my Civic and spoke Setswana out loud to myself, just so I wouldn't forget it completely.

After grad school—partly inspired by my South African friends—I spent a few years working for Maryland Citizen Action Network, a grassroots organization that advocated national health care. I was quickly promoted to canvass director, the person responsible for the door-to-door fundraising program. Though I tired of quotas and the stress of supervising a large and quirky staff, I learned how to talk to strangers and how to run a staff meeting. I also learned more about environmental issues, including the disconcerting concept of "global warming," though at the time it felt more abstract than the environmental problems I could observe myself, like the shocking amount of garbage most of my neighbors set out for the landfill each week.

Nature had always been my refuge. Starting at age five, my mother brought me to Philadelphia's Wissahickon Creek, where my best friend Mary and I roamed the hilly trails as my mother sat on a bench by the creek watching the Canadian geese. In middle school, overnight Girl Scout camp had been my escape from the cramped apartment over the movie theatre. In high school, backpacking along the Appalachian Trail and canoeing in the New Jersey Pine Barrens had grounded me through college applications and editing the yearbook, making those stresses feel much less daunting. I had chosen Duke for its lavish gardens as much as its academics and met Maureen on a freshman bike trip across North Carolina to the Blue Ridge Mountains. Loving the outdoors had seemed as much a part of my identity as my Irish surname and my Roman Catholic upbringing.

In 1981, during spring of my freshman year, I attended Ash Wednesday services in the Duke Chapel. In the middle of the Nicene Creed, I suddenly found myself questioning whether I believed everything I was reciting. It threw me into an anxious week of asking everyone I knew if they believed in God, which most people found disconcerting, if not impolite. I felt no relief from my existential questions until a spring break backpacking trip in the backwoods of the Blue Ridge Mountains. After three days of hiking, our small coed crew of college students split up for a day of "solos," where each person staked out a small piece of wilderness and spent time alone in it. Looking out at the distant, rolling ridges with my journal on my lap, I realized that I did believe there was something greater than my little life, some divine presence, though I sensed it in the woods more often than in church. I felt a calm reassurance that, for now, that was enough.

In Bobonong, I had felt that connection gazing up at the brilliant night sky. Back in the United States, I had sought it through occasional hikes, especially in Virginia's Shenandoah National Park. By my late twenties, I yearned for something less remote. My father had died while I was in grad school, though at the time I avoided feeling much by keeping busy. Now, I was searching for a sense of meaning beyond my activist work and felt the need of a spiritual community. I often missed the forty minutes of weekly silent worship at my high school, which like several private schools in the Philadelphia area was founded by Quakers. I had always liked the little I knew about Quakerism and decided it was time to learn more.

The first Quakers (also called Friends) believed that the religious institutions of seventeenth-century England had lost touch with their spiritual source, so they stripped away anything that distracted them from God—stained glass windows, gold candlesticks, bishops, fashion, and gambling, for starters. They waited in silence in "meeting for worship" to directly experience God without a priest or ordained minister. The "Inward Light" or "Inward Teacher" could be accessed by anyone, they proclaimed, regardless of gender, race, or even religion. In England, they were labeled heretics and thrown in jail by the thousands. In the Massachusetts Bay Colony, four Quakers were hung on Boston Common.

In subsequent centuries, Quakers became known for their work for peace and social justice. Quakers were prominent in the movement to abolish slavery, some provided hiding places on the Underground Railroad. The early women's movement had a disproportionate number of Quaker leaders, and the lead organizer of the famous 1963 March on Washington, Bayard Rustin, was a Quaker. I thought it impressive history for a group that was such a small minority. I was also attracted to the idea that faith was not just something you trotted out on Sunday morning but a compass for how you lived every day.

At twenty-nine, I looked up the local Quaker congregation (called a "meeting"), which was only ten minutes from my house. A middle-aged woman shook my hand as I entered the simple worship room—with no altar or candlesticks, no art or icons, just four groups of wooden benches facing the center of the room. When I sat down in the silence, I glanced around and saw some people with their eyes closed peacefully, others glancing around, like me, smiling when they recognized a friend. Although many people still mistakenly confused Quakers with the Amish, I knew from my high school that most Quakers in the early 1990s didn't dress distinctively. My uniform of jeans, a simple top, and flat shoes fit right in. At the coffee hour afterward, I met a woman who had served in the Peace Corps decades earlier and an American man married to a Kenyan. I felt immediately at home.

I came back the next week, and the next. I liked sitting with others in silence, punctuated occasionally by a "message" from someone who felt moved by the Spirit to stand and speak. By now I was feeling restless and disillusioned with my fundraising job. An hour of Quaker worship each Sunday gave me space to heed the urge to write that was bubbling up within me. On a yellow legal pad, I scribbled out an article on the national health care debate and then typed it up at work. Encouraged when *In These Times* published it, I wondered if there was a way to write full time. I gave my boss several months' notice, though I had no plan for what to do next.

Through a weekend retreat organized by the meeting, I learned about Pendle Hill, a spiritual study center just south of Philadelphia. Founded by Quakers in 1930 as an experiment in nonacademic adult education, Pendle Hill offered a resident program with three ten-week terms per year and courses like, "Writing Your Spiritual Autobiography," "Faith and Feminism," and "Explorations with Clay." As soon as I saw the tree-filled pictures on the brochure, I started telling people I was going before I had even filled out the application or figured out how to pay for a term. When I learned of a private Quaker fund for people who were following "their deepest inward spiritual leadings," I applied and was given twice as much money as I asked for because (miraculously, it seemed to me) the committee sensed I was meant to stay two terms rather than one.

Only a half-hour drive from my mother's apartment, Pendle Hill's twenty-three acres included dawn redwoods, Canadian hemlocks, and a massive three hundred-year-old American beech. Although the night sky wasn't as brilliant as Bobonong's, on a clear night I could see the Big Dipper when I walked from the craft studio back to my dorm room. It was half the size of my old rondavel with a large window overlooking a crab apple tree, a single bed, a small closet, and a sink. The desk was big enough for my first computer, a tan IBM desktop a lawyer friend had given me when she was upgrading. I started writing, saving my work on 5 ¼-inch floppy disks like those I'd used with the Yale computers a few years earlier.

At Pendle Hill I had privacy, though there were other people right outside the door when I wanted company, as in Bobonong. There were communal vacuum cleaners, washing machines, and one television, so I could enjoy modern conveniences without purchasing them. I had a weekly job, cleaning one of the shared bathrooms, and a daily job, washing dishes after lunch, but these took less time than cooking and washing dishes for myself three meals a day would. Although I had hardly sung or played my guitar since the Peace Corps, I started singing in the Pendle Hill choir and playing Celtic tunes with an Englishman who had a fiddle.

Aside from working the occasional weekend at my old catering job to make some cash, I didn't need to drive much since the Pendle Hill kitchen prepared delicious food, often from their own garden, and the library kept me stocked with books, though I did occasionally visit the nearby Borders to buy bite-sized balls of chocolate filled with hazelnut flavoring. Between classes and chores, I walked in the nearby Swarthmore woods. Even more than the tall oaks, I marveled at the fallen trees, their rotting wood sprouting new life. I found myself shaping tree stumps out of clay in my crafts class, fascinated with that image of natural decay and renewal.

The students at Pendle Hill had come for different forms of renewal. One was healing from a painful divorce. A college professor had been denied tenure and was deciding what to do next. Some were exploring their creativity and, like me, wondering if they could make a career out of doing something they loved. Most were on a spiritual search, hoping to find (or in some cases rediscover) their core in the daily meeting for worship or in the crafts studio. One middle-aged man had given up a high-paying business career, drastically reducing his expenses so he could spend his time on prayer and reflection.

A young German man moved the furniture out of his room and slept on a Zen mat, a spinning wheel the only other possession in his room.

He pared down to what seemed to be one pair of jeans and one sweater, though how he managed to do laundry was a mystery no one dared explore. People were accepting of his eccentricity, until his birthday. The Pendle Hill kitchen only served dessert when it was someone's birthday, so chocolate lovers discretely lobbied for a brownie night, while ice cream lovers hinted about how warm it had been lately. When he requested a small cup of nuts and raisins for his special dessert, he received the sort of scorching glares that only sugar-deprived pacifists can deliver.

At Pendle Hill, I thought a lot about what it meant to live simply. After a decade of not reading the Bible, I took the class "Discovering the Gospels Together" and was struck by this teaching from Jesus in the Gospel of Matthew:

> Look at the birds of the air, that they do not sow, nor reap nor gather into barns, and yet your heavenly Father feeds them. . . . And why are you worried about clothing? Observe how the lilies of the field grow; they do not toil nor do they spin, yet I say to you that not even Solomon in all his glory clothed himself like one of these.

I knew from my own experience that when I didn't worry, I always had enough—maybe not enough money to go back to Botswana for Mmadithapelo's wedding, but certainly enough of everything I truly needed.

To find freedom in simplicity, I realized, you had to trust that if you only had one pair of jeans, you'd be okay if they got ripped, that if you didn't stockpile onions, you'd be able to borrow one when you needed to. You had to trust that your worth wasn't measured by what kind of car you drove or whether you owned the latest computer. Living with that kind of trust seemed harder when you felt like an isolated individual, responsible for meeting your own needs. Feeling connected—to a community or to a Higher Power—helped enormously.

I loved the Quaker concept that "way opens"—or circumstances fall into place—when we're on the right path. That had matched my experience, from my unusually rapid acceptance to the Peace Corps to the scholarship I received to attend Pendle Hill for twice as much time as I had originally requested. After two terms as a student, I was recruited to stay on staff and help develop a program on social issues. Because my expenses were so low, I was able to save most of my salary, giving me a buffer when I eventually plunged into full-time writing. It felt like some divine power—which I was starting to feel comfortable calling God—was looking out for me.

When I left Pendle Hill at the end of 1993, I moved into another group house, this time in Pennsylvania's Endless Mountains, part of the Appalachian chain that stretched from Newfoundland to Alabama. Though the surrounding hills were modest compared to the Shenandoah or the North Carolina segment where I had camped during college, I could see Elk Mountain, a winter ski resort, on my daily walk past dairy farms and vacation homes. By my large window, which overlooked a row of hostas along a creek bank, I set up the clunky, hand-me-down computer my lawyer friend had given me a year and a half earlier and started to write my first book.

I was living off of my modest savings when the computer sputtered and died one day, seemingly beyond repair. Before I had time to worry about how I'd finish the book, a friend from Pendle Hill who lived nearby showed up at my door and handed me a $1,000 check to buy a new computer. Sue felt I was following God's guidance, she explained, and wanted to support me, a sentiment that was as meaningful as the money.

Years later, after my mother died and I had extra cash, I offered to repay Sue and called her, by then two time zones away. She said to "pay it forward," to pass the blessing on to someone else. Following an intuition, I offered the $1,000 to another friend, who was writing her first book with no income. When my offer came, I later learned, this friend was so broke she had been measuring out how many meals of oatmeal she had left and praying for the faith to trust that God would provide. I'd had no idea.

The book I was writing was about the challenge of trusting that God would provide a partner if I felt called to marriage and motherhood. I began writing it when I was single, in my early thirties, and just starting to feel ready to "settle down." Miraculously, it seemed, a friendship that began platonically was transformed during the writing of the book. A former Catholic priest who had worked mostly in low-income neighborhoods, Tom was unconcerned about clothes—his or mine—and didn't care if I shaved my legs. Having left the priesthood because he wanted a family, Tom was interested in going back to school to study social work. He was one of the few men I had ever dated who seemed like he'd be happy living in a mud hut, too.

About a year after we started dating, we married in Sue's yard, which was part of a larger property owned by our friends Larry and Laurie. Laurie was nervous when she heard I didn't want to rent a tent, but on our wedding day, the sky was as blue as my intuition had predicted. Tom wore a suit that had been given to him by the widow of one of his parishioners. I wore a plain white Laura Ashley tea dress my mother had bought me for ninety-nine dollars. Instead of gifts, we asked friends to bring flowers, take pictures, or sing at our reception—so without hiring a band, a florist, or a photographer, we ended up with beautiful candid photos and touching performances. The theme of trust popped up in many of the messages that people stood up and shared, including one on how beautiful the homegrown sunflowers were despite the drought that had hit the Endless Mountains that summer.

Our reception was held in a wooden community hall that was so decidedly unpretentious that the men's room had an index card notice in shaky scrawl that said, "Please don't pee on the flour." I thought it was so funny I left it up. Our biggest expense was the catered food, though we had friends set the tables the night before to reduce the cost of hiring help. To cut down on waste, we ordered less fillet, chicken, and grilled vegetables than the caterers said we needed and still created Christmas-in-August when we showed up at a soup kitchen with the most delicious leftovers they had ever received. With ninety-six guests, the whole wedding cost $2,000. In my early thirties, with a new husband and a new career, I thought I had the simplicity thing figured out.

I was wrong.

Chapter Four:
Mama's Gonna Buy . . .

Hush, little baby, don't say a word,
Mama's gonna buy you a mockingbird.
And if that mockingbird won't sing,
Mama's gonna buy you a diamond ring. . . .
—Mother Goose

By the time I handcuffed myself to the White House fence in February of 2013, Tom and I had been married over seventeen years. Along with two teenagers, we had five bedrooms, four cell phones, three laptops, two cars, and a Wii—in short, a lifestyle I couldn't have imagined back in the days when all my possessions fit in the back of my Honda Civic.

Parenting was humbling, eroding my youthful assumption that I could just choose different values from the culture around me, but also humbling in the best sense, teaching me that I was not so different from other people after all. Those college friendships that felt strained when I first came home from the Peace Corps seemed to deepen as conversations about boyfriends and bridal showers were replaced by conversations about childbirth and babies. From the first moment I held my daughter Megan and stroked the wisps of red hair that covered her fontanel, I understood the Tswana proverb "A person is a person because of other people" in a new way. I wanted to give her the moon.

Our simple lifestyle changed in an instant. Aside from the basics, like clothes and diapers, our little family suddenly had play mats, plastic keys, musical mobiles, and enough stuffed animals to fill an ark. It was amazing how many contraptions we were given just to put the baby in: a bouncy chair, a sling she hated, a front pack, a back pack, a Pack 'n Play, a car seat, a lightweight umbrella stroller, and a heavy padded stroller—the HUMMER of all strollers. In hindsight, it seems symbolic that I never wanted a wedding shower but consented to a baby shower.

Our consumption increased at the exact moment when our incomes decreased. Tom was getting his master's in social work while working full time for a small nonprofit that provided low-income housing in Scranton, about half an hour's drive south of where we had gotten married in the Endless Mountains. Before coming to Pendle Hill, he had been a parish priest in a low-income urban neighborhood and had taken a reduced salary each month, not anticipating that he'd one day have dependents. Now, our savings were plummeting by the semester. Living like the lilies of the field seemed like something people should try in their twenties.

The day after Megan came home from the hospital, I got a call from a literary agent who wanted to represent my first book, which was almost finished. A publisher offered the exact amount of money we needed to pay Tom's last tuition bill, reinforcing my trust in way opening. I did the final edits at Wegmans, where I drove at nap time each day since Megan never really got the hang of falling asleep in her crib, and I never got the hang of letting her cry. Once her head flopped over in the car seat, I carried her into the café, bought myself a chocolate rugelach or two, and pulled out my manuscript and a pen. It occasionally occurred to me that driving so much was contributing to global warming—which felt a little more pressing now that I had a child—but since no one around me seemed too alarmed, I shrugged off such thoughts.

After the book was finished and off to the printer, I made parenting my primary occupation, writing only the occasional article for the next several years. Tom supported my decision. To make our finances work, we sold his Toyota Camry and shared my rusty Civic. We lived in a one-bedroom apartment, dressed Megan in hand-me-downs, used cloth diapers, and got our videos from the library rather than the video store—measures that freed me from the pressure to go back to paid work right away. Unlike my mother, I had no desire to stay in an apartment for the rest of my life, or in Scranton for that matter, where neither of us had family. We decided that when Tom finished graduate school, we would move to Philadelphia to be closer to my mom since Tom's mother had eight other children who already lived near her in Wisconsin.

It only took a few math calculations to realize that renting a small place in Philadelphia would be more expensive than buying. We found a 1,045-square-foot house in the East Falls neighborhood of the city, only a fifteen-minute drive from the apartment over the movie theatre. Except for the lack of windows, I liked having a row home, wedged between two other houses with only a wall between us. It kept our heating bills low and made it easy to strike up conversation with neighbors a few doors down in either direction. When the weather was warm, I sat on our front porch with Megan, blowing bubbles or watching people walk their dogs. It wasn't as simple as a rondavel, but with three bedrooms and one bath, our home was modest compared to the homes of friends from Duke, like Maureen, whose second child was a little older than Megan.

With a mortgage (even a relatively small one), mortgage insurance, home insurance, city car insurance, not to mention family health insurance, Tom's social worker salary wasn't quite enough. A few months after our second child, Luke, was born—with brown hair and more energy than a caffeinated puppy—I started teaching an early-morning class, first writing and then eventually South African history, at The University of the Arts. Tom watched the kids while I taught, passing off the car and kids when I walked out of class and he headed to his job advocating for older adults with mental health issues. I tried to keep writing during the kids' nap times, but I wasn't very productive until the children were old enough to be in school full time.

Our finances were manageable but tight. Although I was frugal compared to some families around us, I was never as thrifty as my mother, a high school graduate who took the money she saved reusing her half stockings and invested it in a mix of stocks and Treasury bonds, recording the dividends she received in an old stenographer's notebook. She explained her philosophy by quoting her father, a blacksmith who had only finished the fourth grade in rural County Longford, Ireland. One evening after World War II, when my mother and aunt were still living at home with their parents in Bala Cynwyd, my aunt announced that she had been hearing a lot about these miraculous new gadgets called televisions and wanted to buy one.

My grandfather leaned back from the dinner table and said in his thick brogue, "Don't buy a television. Buy stock in the company that makes the televisions everyone else is buying."

My aunt obeyed and bought stock in RCA. A year later, my mother claims, she sold the stock at such a profit that she was able to buy a coat, a cruise to Europe, and a television.

After my parents' laundry business failed and my mother lost her inheritance, she went to work as a cashier at the Quaker school where I eventually attended high school. She saved every penny she could squirrel away, while my father spent his bartending tips on cigarettes and lottery tickets. After he died, she bought shares of Apple and Intel during the tech boom of the nineties, though she never bought herself an answering machine or VCR, let alone a computer. She kept the same beige, rotary dial phone issued by Ma Bell in 1956 and the apartment over the movie theatre, even as lung disease started to sap her strength and a place without stairs would have been easier.

As her body shriveled and weakened over the course of her eighty-third and final year, my mother's wobbly middle-of-the-night trips to the bathroom made me increasingly nervous, but she refused to wear Depends or a medical alert button, which would at least call someone if she fell. After months of my prodding, she finally agreed to let me hire a nurse's aide to be there when either the hospice workers or I couldn't. I argued that help was a good use of the money she had saved all those years, though she wrote the checks grudgingly, balancing her checkbook to the penny until the day she finally stopped breathing and had to let it all go.

Inheriting my mother's savings made it possible for us to afford more than she could when I was a child, which was a relief since her level of frugality felt impossible. For one thing, I lived in an era where nothing lasted as long as her dial-up phone because manufacturers had figured that making products that broke and needed to be replaced was more profitable than making ones that didn't. From cars and refrigerators to eggbeaters and toasters, our things were always breaking. As a result, we needed a new push-button phone every two years and a new computer every five.

Of course, each new generation of computer was faster and more functional than the last, so I didn't complain when my 5 ¼-inch floppy disks were replaced by 3 ½-inch disks and eventually a flash drive. Unlike my mother, I wanted an answering machine and a VCR, at least until DVDs came along. Although I had been attracted to Tom partly for his simplicity, when he won an iPad as a prize at work and said he might as well give it away since he didn't really need it, I looked at him as incredulously as Luke.

My biggest struggle with simplicity was that I wasn't as good at saying no to my children as my mother had been. She had never thrown me a birthday party—arguing that you should never invite people to an occasion for which they'd feel obliged to bring a gift—but I knew I couldn't be that hard core. We managed to keep Megan's first party, at age three, relatively simple: five guests, a craft project, cheese pizza, and a homemade cake. I had tried to discourage gifts, but when people insisted, I suggested art supplies to go with the easel Megan got from us, which my father had made for me when I was little. When Megan turned four, she asked for an edible Barbie decal on the homemade cake, and I relented, only to have the girls get into a fight over who would get to eat Barbie's face.

As Megan was invited to more birthday parties herself, I started asking parents what they did or didn't want their children to have. Most were surprised by the question. For a while our favorite gift for three-year-old girls was a glittery box of gaudy thrift shop jewelry, which Megan enjoyed just as much as the overpriced Barbie beads at Toys"R"Us. Sometimes we brought the child to a museum as a gift. Some moms seemed to think we were cool and artsy, though I worried some thought I was just cheap. It didn't take long for my children to come to that conclusion. When Megan, at age five, mentioned wanting a piñata for her birthday party and I said enthusiastically that we could make one, she rolled her big brown eyes and said, "Mom, people don't *make* piñatas. They *order* piñatas."

For the next few years, we made our own piñatas out of newspaper, flour, and glue. Luke requested a pirate, then a spider, whose legs were made from empty paper towel rolls painted black, and then Mars, which was surprisingly difficult to make round. Megan asked for a giant daisy, which turned out to be the most involved. I was proud of our creative effort, even if these projects weren't exactly simple, sometimes requiring me to do the last layer in the middle of the night. Eventually my enthusiasm for piñatas was ripped to death by a bunch of nine-year-olds taking turns with a baseball bat, then swarming for the candy like lions on a wildebeest carcass.

On Sundays, the children took turns attending Tom's Catholic church and my Quaker meeting, which I had hoped would help provide a counterbalance to the materialistic mainstream culture. One year, I took Megan to an annual Quaker gathering in Philadelphia. Sitting on the old wooden benches of the enormous meeting room—with never-varnished plank floors, crown-glass windows, and ancient horsehair cushions on the benches—Megan sat and braided colorful friendship bracelets. During a break, our friend Hollister Knowlton walked over to say hello. A woman fourteen years older than I, with short salt-and-pepper hair, Hollister lived more simply than just about any American I knew, eating vegan, taking the bus at all hours, and keeping the heat uncommonly low in her tiny house to reduce her environmental impact.

"Those are beautiful!" Hollister said to Megan.

"They're for sale," said Megan, continuing to braid.

"Oh!" said Hollister, sounding impressed. "Are you raising money for some good cause?"

"No, I'm raising money to buy an iPod," said Megan matter-of-factly. "My mom won't buy me one." In the end, Tom and I agreed to match the money she saved herself on the condition that she didn't play it too loudly or during social situations.

We seemed to develop a regrettable pattern where they begged for something, I said no for as long as I could stand it, and then gave in, just before they lost interest in the item, leaving everyone unsatisfied. First there was the Tamagotchi, a virtual pet shaped like a flattened egg that flew off the Toys"R"Us shelves like they really were alive. Our neighbor Annie, who was the dean of a charter school, collected a desk full of confiscated Tamagotchis during the fad. Since they needed to be electronically fed and walked in order to continue working, the toys all "died" in her desk, each making a different miserable sound as it expired, depending on what type of animal it was supposed to be.

"Nobody's parents wanted the Tamagotchis back," Annie told us with a laugh.

Next there were heelies, the sneakers with wheels that could pop in and out. The schools had to ban those, too. Then there were those rubber bracelets that came in different shapes: a heart, Darth Vader, the Phillies symbol—pretty much anything you can imagine. Each phase was relatively brief. Each time I surrendered to the constant begging about a week before the fad was over. Watching juice boxes, Happy Meals toys, Tamagotchis and heelies fill the trash cans of our middle-class circle made me wonder how much of the world would be covered with landfills by the time my children had children of their own, but that sort of sentiment just made me the preachy, ogre mom.

I knew what it was like to be the only kid who didn't have a birthday party or a Barbie condo. I remembered, as a child, going to my cousins' for Christmas dinner and envying their tree, tall and tinsel-soaked with flashing colored lights, encircled by presents a few feet deep, ripped wrapping paper tossed nearby. In contrast, we had a small, spare tree, and I had to unwrap my one gift carefully so mom could reuse the paper the next year. Perhaps it was because of the bankruptcy, but my mother always said that Santa Claus was a cruel story to tell children because those who got less might think they were less deserving. Years later, I was grateful Tom and I hadn't promoted Santa either when we spent Christmas with a relative whose son got more gifts on Christmas morn than my two children combined.

I knew it was feeling different from other kids that was painful, not the lack of stuff. My students in Bobonong seemed perfectly happy making their own toy bicycles out of wire, but Megan and Luke were comparing themselves to other middle-class American kids, all of whom, they swore, had cable and a cell phone. I had a hard time convincing them that they were not poverty-stricken.

We did manage to hold out on the cell phones longer than the families around us, despite Luke's argument that someday he might be in a life-threatening situation and need a phone with GPS. What was interesting to me was how parents and children alike had become convinced within the matter of a few years that cell phones were necessary for children's safety, even though when kids in Philadelphia got mugged it always seemed to be for their cell phones. The thing I objected to was not the phones themselves—which are wonderful inventions that I got hooked on as soon as I finally purchased one myself—it was being told that something was a necessity when I knew perfectly well that it was possible to survive without one.

I could see I was going to be swimming against the tide, subverting the capitalist growth imperative by teaching my children to question how much they needed. Each summer we had a debate over the school supply list, which always included pencils, markers, notebooks, and a ruler. Megan and Luke were adamant that they needed new pencils each August—"But the list says pencils!"—despite the five pounds of slightly used pencils that languished in a plastic tub in the coat closet. They were unimpressed by my description of students in Bobonong using each pencil down to the nub. They turned up their noses at the previous year's half-used notebooks. Eventually I got the bright idea to bribe them fifty cents for every object they salvaged, which was less expensive for me than buying everything new and kept last year's binders out of the landfill.

I had mixed feelings about holding up my students in Bobonong as the ideal of simplicity since using each pencil down to the nub had been a necessity, not a lifestyle choice. I first realized the danger in the way I portrayed my African village when my children were in nursery school, and their teacher asked me to speak to the class about my time in the Peace Corps. Even at three or four, the children had already absorbed a stereotypical picture of Africa from *The Lion King* and *Madagascar*, not to mention the pre-K teacher who introduced the continent with a large picture of a lion. My story of living in a mud hut seemed to reinforce an image of backwardness, even though I tried to explain that my rondavel was cooler than the cinder block houses that were considered more modern. Another year when I visited a class, I overheard two first-grade boys looking at a photo. One commented knowingly, "You can tell they're Africans because they are not wearing any shoes."

From then on, when teachers asked me to come speak to their class, I mixed my old village photos with pictures of the middle-class suburbs of Lagos and African men in business suits talking on their cell phones.

"*All* of these are images of Africa," I emphasized, pointing out the wide range of skin tones and lifestyles found across the continent.

Even though the blue airmail letters from Botswana had dried up over the years, I still thought of Botswana often, especially Mmadithapelo. When I'd seen her for the last time in 1986, she had said, "Eileen, I love you, but I'm a terrible correspondent. You're never going to hear from me."

It was true she wasn't a great writer, but for several years I'd received the occasional letter, an invitation to her wedding, which I was too broke to attend, and a picture of her son and daughter, who were a few years older than mine. The last letter I'd received said, "I'm having some troubles in my life," ominous coming from a woman in Botswana, where HIV/AIDS had skyrocketed since my departure. I wrote back, gingerly asking how she was. After several unanswered letters, I'd feared the worst.

Then, on a whim one day a few years later, I'd searched for Mmadithapelo on Facebook and found someone with her surname who turned out to be from Bobonong. This young woman was a toddler when I was there in the eighties, when the village had no reliable phone service and no electricity, except for small generators at the clinic, the chief's house, and the bar. Now, in the first decade of the twenty-first century, Bobonong had a Facebook group. Sitting with my laptop in a Philadelphia coffee shop, I sent the young woman a message and was thrilled to receive a quick reply. I delicately mentioned Mmadithapelo and asked if she knew her.

"She's my auntie!" came the immediate response. "She is living in Orapa." Within minutes we had exchanged several messages where I impressed her by remembering some Setswana, and she promised to get me her aunt's contact info. I was elated.

"You won't believe what just happened!" I said to the baristas at the coffee shop where I was working, trying to convey both the miracle of chatting live with someone from Bobonong and my relief that my friend had not died of AIDS. I continued telling the story to everyone I ran into for the next several days.

About a week later, I found a cryptic message on my home answering machine from Mmadithapelo: "I was just thinking about you, Eileen. I'm not dead." Click.

When she called back a few hours later, I exclaimed, "Your niece told you about meeting me on Facebook!"

Mmadithapelo sounded confused. She had never heard of Facebook and didn't know which niece I meant. She had simply been thinking of me—during the week when I was talking so much about her. She felt bad that she hadn't written in several years, so she picked up her cell phone and called a number that I didn't even realize she had. We inquired after each other's children, talked about how much Bobonong had changed since they finished the tar road, and promised to stay in better touch. She never did explain what made her say, "I'm not dead," as if she suspected that I thought she was.

I was amazed that I could now connect to people all over the world through my wireless laptop and staggered by how much Botswana had changed over the course of a generation, but none of these human-made changes felt as miraculous as the invisible network of love that bound friends across time and continents. I'd thought of Mmadithapelo—had almost conjured her—and she called.

In the years since I lived in Bobonong, I'd never had a next-door neighbor like Mmadithapelo—someone I could borrow an onion or an egg from without awkwardness or obligation—until Annie and Will moved next door. We were friendly with many of our neighbors, but Will and Annie were special. For starters, Will had two children, William and Kayla, who stayed with him on Wednesdays and alternate weekends. As William and Kayla became friends with Megan and Luke, my children developed a new and delightful pastime: going outside to play, which I had never managed to promote as long as their best friends lived a car ride away. Now play was as simple as riding bikes in loops around the block or acting out Ninjas on the sidewalk. Sometimes the girls painted their nails and the boys played electric guitar. Sometimes the adults sat out on our porch steps and talked about politics, Will's travels as a musician, or Annie's adventures as a charter school dean.

With my mother gone—and Tom, Will, and Annie's families far away—we started celebrating holidays together when we were all in town. On Christmas, Will sat down at the piano and played whatever carol was requested, whether he knew it or not, following the children as they belted out a tune. One summer we parents planned a joint camping trip that we managed to keep secret from the kids despite the fact that we were packing our cars the same morning. Megan and Luke were told they were going to Niagara Falls, while William and Kayla were told they were going to Canada, and no one's grasp of geography was good enough to suspect a thing. The joy on their faces when they saw each other at the campground and realized we were at adjoining sites beat that on any Christmas morning.

Being good friends with our next-door neighbors had many fringe benefits. I borrowed chairs when I was hosting a gathering of Quaker bloggers and came back for dish detergent when we discovered we were out. Because we had a more convenient spigot, Annie used our back yard hose to water her tomatoes and zucchini. When we were three hours late getting home from an afternoon hiking trip, she used her spare key to let herself in and walk our mutt, Spud. When half their Mulberry tree fell into the alley one summer while they were away, I called Will to let them know, then e-mailed a photo to assure him his gas grill was unharmed.

It was almost like living in a village.

Chapter Five:
The Seventh Generation

*In every deliberation, we must consider the impact on the
seventh generation . . . even if it requires having
skin as thick as the bark of a pine.*
—Great Law of the Iroquois

The famous Iroquois admonition to consider the impact of our decisions on the next seven generations felt a lot less abstract after having children. I'd read Bill McKibben's groundbreaking book *The End of Nature* when Luke was a baby. I had gradually accepted that human-caused greenhouse gases were warming our atmosphere, though just when I got used to the term "global warming," scientists started calling it "climate change" to include the many other problems caused by a warming planet—droughts, floods, hurricanes, disappearing species, and rising sea levels, to name a few. I'd seen Al Gore's film *An Inconvenient Truth* with its big, scary-looking graphs. Like many others, I wondered what it would mean to my children's future.

At the same time, I felt a little internal resistance whenever I heard predictions that sounded alarmist. By 2008, *The New York Times* was reporting a possible "tipping point" in the Arctic, where melting ice was raising sea levels and releasing methane, which would further add to greenhouse gases, exacerbating the problem. One scientist quoted in the article said, "We're moving beyond a point of no return." Others were using the term "catastrophic climate change." Surely it wasn't going to be *that* bad, I secretly thought to myself—Y2K had blown over, wouldn't this?

In addition to feeling skeptical, I felt powerless to do much. I knew that Western levels of consumption contributed a disproportionate amount of greenhouse gases, but if the problem was really "catastrophic," using compact florescent bulbs and recycling just didn't feel like enough. It seemed fitting that the year's most popular movies—*The Dark Knight, Twilight, Iron Man,* and *The Incredible Hulk*—were all stories where men with superpowers protected everyone else from some personified evil. It was an appealing fantasy.

Still, I couldn't put the dire environmental predictions totally out of mind. I often thought of dry Botswana as I poured the water collected in the dehumidifier down the basement utility sink. One day, in a moment of zeal, I decided that I should just carry it upstairs and use it to water the plants or flush the toilet. That lasted a few days. For a few weeks, I tried taking the kids to piano lessons by bus, but it took forty-five minutes and six dollars each way, so I resumed the ten-minute drive. Resigned to needing a car, we bought a Prius, but a minor accident totaled the delicate electronics. Given how easily the Prius had crumpled and how quickly our children were approaching driving age, we decided to replace it with a sturdier Camry. For me, the saddest part of going back to a less fuel-efficient vehicle was that I no longer appeared to others like the person I imagined myself to be.

In the summer of 2008, Luke and I took the train across Pennsylvania to a national gathering of over a thousand Quakers, where limiting our environmental impact was a hot topic. While struggling to pack a manageable bag, I considered bringing my travel coffee mug but instead packed a stack of pamphlets I'd written for an interest group on parenting and spirituality. The first morning of the gathering, I went to get a cup of coffee in the crowded dining hall and looked around for a ceramic mug, only to find Styrofoam. Returning to my table with my politically incorrect cup, I passed a middle-aged Quaker with a ceramic mug.

"Excuse me, where did you find that?" I asked.

"*I* brought *mine* from home," she said with what I heard as excessive smugness.

I gritted my teeth and started drafting a defensive internal monologue on the way back to my table: Hey, Smug Mug Lady, I packed light because I took the train with a kid. I care about the environment, too! If you go around judging everyone, you're not going to be a very effective agent for change. When I told someone the story that afternoon, I still sounded bitter.

Although I bristled when I felt criticized for my consumption, it was partly because I felt conflicted myself. A few months after the Quaker conference, I decided to try a new approach. Since the production and transportation of food used a lot of water and fuel, I decided to try eating just a little less. I didn't starve myself. I just had half a baked potato at dinner instead of a whole one, or a medium tortilla instead of large when we were having burritos. To my delight, ten excess pounds slid off easily. I felt great getting back into my most flattering pair of black pants, which hadn't fit since the stressful year my mother died.

Appreciating the compliments I was getting, I thought it would be great to lose ten more pounds, which would put me back to my pre-parenting weight in the middle of the "healthy" column on the medical weight charts. To get a little help, I visited a hypnotist who advertised Weight Loss on the sign I had driven past for years. When I finally ventured into his office, he showed me a video of testimonials and tried to pressure me into signing up for an expensive, ten-week weight-loss hypnosis series. He scoffed when I mentioned that not wanting to eat more than my fair share of the world's food was helping to motivate me. I left his office feeling ridiculed and comforted myself with a Starbucks hot chocolate with whipped cream. Within a few months, I had gained all the weight back.

By 2009, the United States was in recession and dragging down much of the world along with it. President Obama, who had talked about climate change on the campaign trail, was now focused on stimulating the economy—bailing out the banks and the auto industry, encouraging Americans to buy new cars, and defending himself from critics on the right. Climate change had disappeared from his lexicon.

That summer, I attended a panel discussion on "Earthcare" at a regional gathering of a few hundred Quakers. The first panelist was social change trainer George Lakey, a tall man with white hair and a booming voice, who said something I would never forget: "If we are really serious when we say that climate change is going to be catastrophic, then shouldn't we be acting more courageously and effectively to address it?"

As a young white man from a Pennsylvania slate mining town, George had joined the civil rights movement in the early 1960s. He'd been trained in nonviolent direct action and had been arrested in a city hall sit-in. Nearly fifty years later, he spoke passionately about the need to use similar tactics today. He was not talking about the kind of bland vigils and rallies I had found disheartening after the invasion of Iraq because they had no strategy and no impact. He was talking about actually challenging the powers that be in ways that had worked for people like Gandhi and Martin Luther King, Jr. Many people were inspired.

"I'm ready to hear the most radical thing you can say to us about what we have to do," said a tall redheaded man who was about my age during the question and answer period.

"Show me the way," implored a younger man, who noted he would be heading home in a gas-fueled vehicle to a busy life.

I was moved by the Earthcare panel and thought of it a few weeks later while kayaking with Hollister, the vegan friend who had admired Megan's friendship bracelets a few years earlier. Her family owned a summer home on a tranquil lake in the Adirondack Mountains. We had paddled from that lake through a narrow inlet full of lily pads and toads to an even more pristine lake completely devoid of houses or motorboats. Tamarack, hemlock, and pine enveloped the long, glittering slice of water, which bore no obvious signs of human presence except for one wooden dock that anchored a trailhead. I let my kayak drift, the paddle laid across my lap, as I quietly watched a pair of loons floating not far away.

This little piece of wilderness had been preserved since the 1890s by the Adirondack League Club, founded by wealthy industrialists who had wanted to protect the place for their own hunting and fishing. I felt grateful that our family was able to experience this peaceful, wild refuge, but I wondered how these 53,000 acres would fare in the century to come. How would rising temperatures affect the loons or the tamarack, a cold-loving conifer that lined the shores? It wasn't just polar bears whose habitat was changing.

I remembered George Lakey's talk challenging Quakers to address climate change with the kinds of tactics used during the civil rights movement and tried to imagine what that might look like. What would be the contemporary equivalent to the segregated Woolworths lunch-counters, where black students were arrested in 1960 for ordering a cup of coffee? Many others had boycotted Woolworths, but boycotting fossil fuels seemed impossible today, given the way our society was structured. With climate change, the line between victim and perpetrator felt fuzzier and the solutions more elusive. How could we decrease greenhouse emissions when capitalism demanded endless consumption? And it wasn't just capitalism as some abstract system, but we the customers, who always wanted the newest MacBook Pro or iPhone. Who were the targets, if not ourselves?

Floating on the lake, I decided to write an article about these questions for *The Washington Post*'s online edition, an opportunity my publicist at Tarcher/Penguin had arranged to publicize my second book, which was about to be released. The book was on the Serenity Prayer—which asks for serenity to accept the things we cannot change, courage to change the things we can change, and wisdom to know the difference—and I figured it wasn't a stretch to relate this to the changes we needed to make to slow climate change. When I called George to interview him for the article, I told him my concern about finding a target comparable to segregated lunch counters since our own excessive consumption contributed to our society's high carbon emissions.

"Social transformation has always involved changing ourselves and changing institutions," he explained patiently. He gave the example of confronting his own racism as a white man, even while getting arrested at civil rights sit-ins in the sixties. "Today, we might take the bus more, while holding accountable the powers that killed the electric car," he said. "We might take shorter showers, while challenging the financial interests that undermine the development of renewable energy." The idea that changing my own consumption was only part of the equation planted a little seed of hope, though it took a few more years to germinate.

When my talks and workshops on the Serenity Prayer were winding down, I read Mark Hertsgaard's book *Hot: Living Through the Next*

Fifty Years on Earth. A science reporter who'd covered climate change for decades, Hertsgaard said he didn't really "get it" until he became a parent and imagined the future of his young daughter, who was growing up along a piece of California coast that might be underwater in fifty years. Throughout the book he used his innocent little daughter—featured in his book-jacket photo—to make climate change personal, wagering that wanting what's best for our children would help readers overcome their fear and denial. As a parent, I found it an effective strategy.

Certainly some of what he shared was fear-inspiring: water shortages alternating with floods, millions of refugees, famine . . . and those were the inevitable problems, not the worst-case scenarios. What I appreciated about *Hot* was that Hertsgaard also told stories of hope and action: governments, corporations, and citizens working for creative solutions; US mayors planting trees in low-income neighborhoods, knowing that the poor are more vulnerable to rising summer temperatures; West African farmers using innovative techniques to shade their crops, adapting to climate change while mitigating its strength by reducing carbon.

While Hertsgaard did not sugarcoat the task ahead of us if we wanted to avoid the worst possible climate change scenarios, he also offered possibilities that I found surprisingly encouraging. He asserted that if every sidewalk in the United States and the roof of every house were painted white or silver, it would have the same climate effect as taking all US automobiles off the road. It sounded too good to be true, but I wanted to believe. The last time our tar roof had been recoated, the roofer had automatically used silver reflective coating, which he said would help keep us cooler in the summer by reflecting away the sun's heat. I was thrilled to learn that it also combated climate change.

I got on Google Earth and scrolled around the aerial view of our neighborhood to see how many homes had reflective roofs. The line of row homes looked like a jumbled piano keyboard, with about half black and half white keys. Maybe this was the thing I could do, I thought: get my neighbors to paint their roofs, which would also help mitigate the humid Philadelphia summers. There seemed to be a lot of potential for having a big impact without people having to actually change their lifestyles too much.

I wrote a blog post extolling the virtues of reflective roofs. Then I casually asked Annie if they had coated their roof lately—knowing from Google Earth that it was dark when the last satellite image was taken. She said she didn't think so, and I found myself soft peddling the reflective roof idea, not wanting to sound like the Smug Mug Lady. Within a few days, my enthusiasm for organizing a community-wide effort faded. In between blogging, teaching, grading papers, cooking dinner, keeping track of Megan and Luke, and volunteering at my Quaker meeting, it was hard to imagine myself knocking on my neighbors' doors trying to convince them to pay to prematurely recoat their dark roofs, so I let the idea slip away with a little regret.

Next I attended a workshop at my Quaker meeting on how to teach others how to insulate their houses, but I felt as competent with a caulk gun as I would with a scalpel. Although I liked public speaking and the program's emphasis on helping low-income people save money as well as energy, leading workshops on insulation didn't quite seem like my calling either. Still, I kept feeling like I should be doing more, unable to shake off one point in Hertsgaard's book—his prediction of increased famine.

Despite studying Irish history in college, I didn't know much about my own relatives who had survived the Great Hunger. After reading *Hot*, I dug out a family tree I had stored in our basement after my mother died. According to the notes typed by my mother's second cousin, my great-great-grandparents, Patrick and Rose McEnroe, married in 1846, one year into the five-year famine. They had five children before Patrick died at age thirty, leaving Rose to raise her brood in County Cavan—which lost 50 percent of its population in those years to a combination of starvation, disease, and emigration, according to a book from my local library. Our family's village, I learned, was literally erased from the map.

I could barely imagine the shame and anxiety of watching the walls of your home dismantled, the roof burned, the stones scattered—which may well have happened to my father's people, those who came to the United States on coffin ships to work in the Pennsylvania coal mines. It was even harder to imagine the experience of my mother's family—the ones who continued living in Ireland through the crisis, who shushed their children as a neighbor's house was demolished or as a sister died of hunger, the ones who clung to the place as it disappeared from the map. I wondered how that experience had affected those children and their descendants.

Through a genealogical website, I found the 1901 Irish census, which included the next generation, Patrick and Rose's son James and his wife, Ellen. Elegant cursive script listed their occupations—farmer and housewife—along with their ages and the children who were still at home. Scrolling to the far right of the document, almost by accident, I noticed a column for extra notes. Ellen McEnroe—my mother's mother's mother—was marked as a "lunatic."

I jumped in my chair and reread the notation again and again, imagining possible explanations, but the census concentrated on mundane details, like the fact that the family's roof was temporary—presumably thatch—rather than more expensive and durable slate. I wondered if my great-grandmother was driven to lunacy by raising nine kids in three rooms. ("Rooms, not bedrooms," I emphasized when I told my own children.) Of course, this explanation may have reflected my disposition more than hers. Maybe she was simply menopausal or spirited in an era when diagnosing mental illness was as subjective as reading tea leaves. On the 1911 census a decade later, the "lunatic" box was unchecked.

Hearing the story, an academic friend recommended a beautifully written ethnography called *Saints, Scholars, and Schizophrenics: Mental Illness in Rural Ireland* in which anthropologist Nancy Scheper-Hughes described an aesthetic people, remarkable for their ability to suppress emotion, exemplifying frugality and self-denial, the very qualities that had helped my mother to accumulate the money I'd inherited. Scheper-Hughes recounted several factors that contributed to the high rates of mental illness among the rural Irish, noting in the preface to the twentieth-anniversary edition that with hindsight she "would put a great deal more emphasis on the cumulative effects of the Great Hunger."

In other words, a catastrophic event in the 1840s was still affecting people when she did her research in the 1970s, which made me consider again the Iroquois teaching about the seventh generation. My great-grandmother Ellen, I realized with a shudder as I looked at the dates, was born before the grass had even settled over the unmarked famine graves. When I phoned my mother's second cousin, who had started the family tree, he told me that Ellen's youngest daughter had committed suicide at nineteen, though I'd never heard a word about it from my mother, her niece.

My mother, Helen, was parsimonious when it came to clothing and housing, but unstinting when it came to food. An excellent cook, she always bought the best-quality ingredients: meat from the butcher down the street wrapped in paper before our eyes; unshelled peas fresh from the farmer's market; a block of parmesan, not the pre-shredded stuff in the green canister. One day when I was sixteen, my dad dug into a small jar of fancy raspberry preserves my mother had purchased specially for a raspberry mocha cake recipe she'd found, and I was surprised when she didn't scold him.

"My mother taught me that feeding her family is the highest duty of a wife and mother," she'd explained simply.

That sentiment hit me more sharply now that I realized what a deep shadow the Hunger must have cast over my grandmother's upbringing. I cringed thinking again of Mark Hertsgaard's predictions about famine caused by climate change.

Hollister had told me about a new group called Earth Quaker Action Team, which had formed in response to George Lakey's challenge to address climate change with nonviolent direct action. For their first target, EQAT (pronounced "equate") had selected Pennsylvania-based PNC Bank, which bragged about being "green," while being a top US financier of companies practicing mountaintop removal coal mining. PNC also had Quaker roots, so many Quaker institutions had accounts there, potentially giving EQAT greater leverage. When my own Quaker meeting started discussing whether we should move our money out of PNC, I learned that mountaintop removal contributed to high rates of cancer and birth defects in Appalachia, while burning coal contributed to asthma in places like Philadelphia and climate change everywhere.

I had vaguely thought of checking out Earth Quaker Action Team, but my first involvement with the group came through serendipity—or maybe you could say it was way opening, or God giving me a kick in the butt. I found myself with a strong urge to attend the annual Philadelphia Flower Show, which my mother used to bring me to when I was a child. I e-mailed a friend who liked to go, but it was Ash Wednesday, and she was going to church that morning, so I tried another friend and then another, getting the same response. The idea that I should go that Wednesday stayed with me, so I took the train downtown alone to get into the packed convention center, which housed what was described as "the world's largest indoor flower show."

At first I wasn't sure why I was there. Other than the enormous Eiffel Tower base, I could hardly see the elaborate exhibits for all the women shuffling slowly around them. I craned my neck over what seemed to be mostly white hair to get a glimpse of a field of tulips or a turkey made of flowers and wire, but the sweet smell of flowers felt contrived in this man-made convention center. Then, as I pushed through the crowd, I passed my friend Walter Hjelt Sullivan and a young woman who was interning for a Quaker environmental justice program. They were acting slightly furtive, but Walter whispered to me as he passed, "Meet us at the PNC display at noon—and pray for us." I opened my mouth to ask a question, and he added, "Leave if the police tell you to."

Earth Quaker Action Team was planning an action in twenty minutes, I realized with excitement, just enough time for me to see the Bonsai exhibit before coming back to support the group. It suddenly made sense that they were there since PNC Bank was one of the major sponsors of the Philadelphia Flower Show. At noon I looked for PNC's orange triangular logo in the middle of the crowded convention center and saw that EQAT had already set up a "crime scene" with yellow police tape. Suited security people with walkie-talkies scrambled to figure out what to do with the nine people behind the tape, who stood shoulder to shoulder joyously singing, "Where Have All the Flowers Gone?" in black T-shirts that read, "Flower Crimes Division."

Security recruited the nearby roving jazz band to play in front of the row of singing protesters, who had moved on to "She'll Be Coming Round the Mountain." But the saxophone only brought more attention to the activists, who were asking that PNC's regional president come down to the flower show and address the fact that his bank's investments in mountaintop removal coal mining were destroying flowers, mountains, and communities, while PNC was trying to pass itself off as a green bank and good corporate citizen by funding fields of indoor tulips. While flower show security was caught off guard, Earth Quaker Action Team had clearly prepared for this moment, printing T-shirts just for the occasion, and training people in where to stand and what to do.

The nine people behind the yellow tape, I learned, were prepared to stay if the police asked them to leave, even if that meant getting arrested. It was a way of demonstrating the strength of their convictions by taking a risk and being willing to bear the consequences. I was impressed by the confidence and apparent joy of those risking arrest as they waited for the Philadelphia police to arrive. A few down the row from my friend Walter was the redheaded man who had spoken after George's lecture a year and a half earlier. "I'm ready to hear the most radical thing you can say to us about what we have to do," he'd said. It seemed he was now doing it.

While everyone waited to see whether the police would decide to make arrests, EQAT members on the other side of the yellow tape chatted with the puzzled crowd. I took a stack of the small flyers and started handing them out, pleased to see that most people who paused were supportive, or at least interested in learning about the issue. Only one woman said to me disapprovingly, "Some of us come to the flower show to have a good time!" which it later occurred to me was probably true of the white people who frequented the Greensboro Woolworth in 1960, only to be inconvenienced by those who refused to leave the segregated lunch counters until everyone was able to be served a cup of coffee.

The most interesting thing for me was to observe how exhilarated I felt. I was suddenly grateful that I had come to the flower show alone because it meant I was free to stay for an extra hour to support the group. When I left to catch the train home, the Earth Quakers were still standing strong as the police loitered nearby, apparently reluctant to make a bigger scene by arresting anyone. The sense that I'd been meant to be there was confirmed when I blogged about the experience afterwards and got enthusiastic responses from the EQAT members whom I knew. Writing might be one way for me to do something about climate change, I thought.

Soon afterwards I had the idea to write a book called *The Blessings of a Small House*. I took one of Luke's half-used composition notebooks to the backyard Adirondack chair that Tom and the kids had given me one Mother's Day. Sitting in the shady corner by the fern, I scribbled several pages of ideas and a rough outline. The book would be both personal and political, pointing out that a modest row home like our own gave us greater freedom and lower heating bills than the larger homes and mortgages that were crippling many Americans in the wake of the financial crisis of 2008. I wouldn't say you had to live in a shed in the woods, made of old pallets or milk cartons, the kind of place with no room for a changing table or a piano. I would advocate a modest scaling back of the American trend toward larger and larger houses.

In the next few weeks, I wrote a really terrific first twelve pages and a more detailed chapter outline that included the greater environmental impact of larger homes, but balanced that with the financial self-interest I assumed would motivate most Americans. My literary agent liked the idea, and it felt like it might be the next project for me except for one little problem: Tom and I were thinking of buying a bigger house. Although my first two books had been about listening inwardly for divine guidance, I really wasn't sure what to do.

Chapter Six:
Quiet Desperation

The mass of men live lives of quiet desperation.
—Henry David Thoreau

In that American bible of simplicity, *Walden*—which I had read in high school but didn't understand at the time—Henry David Thoreau explored the lot of his New England neighbors, most of whom spent their days doing work they hated to pay for things they didn't need. Thoreau argued that Native Americans who lived in wigwams they owned themselves were better off than the white men who lived in debt, laboring for decades to pay off larger homes "because they think that they must have such a one as their neighbors have."

Certainly I knew people in the early twenty-first century who were trapped by their mortgages. If they were fortunate enough to be employed, many spent their working hours earning enough money to repay the bank and spent their weekends mowing the lawn and cleaning the bathrooms. Paying bills, answering e-mail, and caring for elderly parents if they had them swallowed the rest of their free time. Thoreau's verdict in 1854—"The mass of men live lives of quiet desperation"—didn't seem outdated except in its exclusion of women.

Yet, despite how much we loved our neighbors and our low heating bills, despite my growing concern about climate change and the book I wanted to write about the benefits of a small house, I often found myself looking wistfully at homes with more windows and larger gardens.

Maybe Thoreau was right, and I just assumed I should have what other people had, but I couldn't quite shake my fantasy of a bigger, more elegant house, even if I did know the downsides. I knew that Will and Annie had a similar fantasy, especially since they were hoping to give William and Kayla younger siblings. Whenever William hinted that they'd be moving some day, I eyed the lawns I passed in nearby Mount Airy and Chestnut Hill, fantasizing about the raised beds I would erect on them.

A bigger vegetable garden was one of the things I most wanted from a bigger house, as well as another bathroom to get us through the teenage years. I also wanted my own office, remembering Virginia Woolf's assertion that a woman needed "a room of her own" in order to write. Tom wanted a quiet space where he could sit and read away from the television and kitchen radio, and a guest room so his family could visit without needing a hotel. As Megan approached high school, we both liked the idea of creating a place where our children would feel comfortable bringing their friends, something I'd never had in the apartment over the movie theatre. Often when I sat down to write, I found myself searching the newest neighborhood listings online, clicking through the staged photos even when I knew the house was out of our price range.

Each Thursday morning I met my friend Deb, and we walked along Philadelphia's Wissahickon Creek, only a few miles from the place my mother had brought me as a child. Deb was my spiritual companion, another working mother of two, who was trying to finish her dissertation in childhood studies while teaching and parenting. Each week we took turns sharing our struggles as we walked under a canopy of ash and maple in a loop down to the creek and back up a stony hill.

"I just really want a bigger garden," I told Deb, slightly out of breath from the hill. "We can't fit any more vegetables in our yard."

"Uh huh," said Deb unconvinced.

Deb felt burdened by a cute house with a large weed-filled yard and a carriage house she and her husband Dave rented to tenants, who always seemed to call with a broken faucet just when she had a dissertation chapter due. On top of university teaching and driving to baseball games, she felt pressured to finish her PhD and get a job to help pay the bills, a reminder of how much more freedom I felt because we had paid off our mortgage with some of my mother's money. Whenever I chafed at the lack of space around the desk in our bedroom, I remembered that it wouldn't do me much good to have a room of my own if I had no time to write in it because of greater financial pressure.

Although I had written more than once about peace as a hallmark of spiritual decision making, I wasn't at peace myself. None of the houses we visited seemed right, but every time I felt ready to just stay in our modest row home, Tom stopped by another open house, stirring up my ambivalence again. One evening, I was sitting on our queen-sized bed while Tom was gathering papers from the IKEA desk I'd gotten for graduate school. It was tucked into the nook between the closet and one of two windows, each with a plant hanging to one side. There was about three feet on my side of the bed, less on Tom's side. We were talking about the house hunt again, and I was recounting the flaws of every house we had seen.

"I guess I'm just resigned," Tom said with deep disappointment in his voice.

"What do you mean?" I asked.

"We're never going to move," he said. "It's just never going to happen."

Tom was an introvert who had been single for forty-two years before plunging into family life. As a hospice social worker, he spent all day with dying people and their families, many in low-income communities with complicated problems; he deserved to have one quiet place, I thought. Moreover, he was the kind of guy who didn't ask for much. Meanwhile, he emphasized that I deserved to have my own office, an argument that made me start to notice how everyone left their crap on my desk. I didn't even have a desk of my own, let alone a room of my own. I headed back to the Internet to search the real estate listings again.

There was one more possible house in our neighborhood, which I had initially dismissed for being on too busy an intersection. On second look, I realized what a nice enclosed yard it had and how close a walk it was to the high school Megan would attend the next year. There were beautiful hydrangeas that flanked the front door, just outside the living room and dining room windows. On the right side, just beyond a glass enclosed porch, there stood a huge rhododendron that almost reached the window of the master bedroom on the second floor. To the left of the house was a small grass hill just far enough from the sidewalk to make it perfect for the raspberries I hoped to transplant from our current yard.

For the first time, we walked into a house that felt like it could actually be home. I could imagine our upright piano fitting in the living room to the left of the fireplace. I could imagine my mother's bamboo furniture all fitting into the master bedroom and my IKEA bookshelves in the small office. Tom could read in the enclosed porch that faced the rhododendron. For the first time, the children seemed excited about the prospect of more space and immediately started arguing over who would get the room with the enormous closet, which Megan wanted for her clothes and Luke wanted because it wrapped around the chimney in a way that made for a great hiding place. After a second visit, we made an offer.

The house was listed as a "short sale," which I learned was a means of avoiding foreclosure that had become much more common since the 2008 financial crisis collapsed housing prices. Assuming that houses always increased in value, many Americans had bought homes they could barely afford, much bigger than the ones their parents had saved for, with larger utility bills and greater upkeep. Banks cleaned up during the boom, and when the whole igloo melted, they got bailed out to the tune of $700 billion. Homeowners were not so lucky. In 2009, a record 2.82 million homes went into foreclosure.

Some struggling homeowners tried to negotiate their way out of the mess, like the people who owned the house we wanted. After failing to sell the house themselves, they had applied to their lender for a short sale, meaning the bank would agree to accept less than what they were owed. Theoretically it was a good deal for everyone. The homeowners would get out of an expensive mortgage. The bank would get more than they would in a foreclosure sale and would avoid taking possession of one more property that would sit empty for months developing basement mold and God knows what else. It sounded like a good deal for us, too. We would get a nice house at a price we could afford. The only hitch was that the bank had to approve the deal, which ended up taking seven frustrating months.

While we waited, I decided to get rid of stuff, whether or not we moved. Over the years, I'd spent thousands of dollars on things that we eventually gave away, from the Tamagotchis and heelies to tennis racquets and books. I'd held onto old Christmas gifts—Megan's dusty microscope and Luke's dusty electric guitar—hoping they would be rediscovered. I knew we weren't the only people who had accumulated so much. My college friend Maureen joked with her husband Mark that they'd never get divorced because they had a deal that whoever left first got stuck with all the junk in the basement. Another friend started a business helping people to clear out their possessions, especially when they were getting ready to move. People paid her good money to get rid of stuff for which they had paid good money.

When my mother died, I had inherited the beautiful bamboo furniture set that her mother had received as a wedding gift from the wealthy family my grandmother served as a maid. Most of my mother's other possessions were things I didn't want: stacks of aluminum pie plates, silk scarves, piles of necklaces made of colored crystal beads, cracked rubber bands, a huge oval painting of the Sacred Heart with a knife through it, and cashmere sweaters with holes in the elbows. There was a drawer with unused wedding gifts, a silver plate and a silver gravy boat, both in their boxes with cards from names I didn't recognize. There was an assortment of ashtrays with shamrocks on them, though no one had smoked since my dad died seventeen years earlier. I spent weeks trying to find new homes for as many things as possible. I didn't want to throw the bloody Sacred Heart in the trash but didn't know anyone who would want it either.

Vowing not to leave my own children such a task, I headed down to our basement closets, but when I pulled out the first musty box, I was unable to get rid of the letters friends and former students had written me from Botswana. If I ever went back, I thought, I'd be able to use those twenty-year-old Setswana language books, so I put them back in the box, too. I'd prided myself on speaking Setswana better than most Peace Corps volunteers, and now I only remembered a few stock phrases that I occasionally practiced in the car. If I couldn't speak the language any more, did that mean that I was no longer that young adventurer? If I held onto the books, could I still claim her as myself?

This was part of the reason we wanted a bigger house. We'd bought electric guitars and microscopes, but we hadn't gotten rid of the bike I rode across North Carolina before my freshman year of college or Tom's theology books from seminary. Now I also had many of my parents' things: the wooden camel my father brought back from Suez when he worked for the Merchant Marines in the 1950s and my mother's small Irish harp with the broken strings. At least we used my grandmother's serving platters on holidays. My mother's manual eggbeater came in handy when our electric one started smoking. It worked so well, in fact, we hadn't bothered to replace the electric one. Still, I wondered where it would end. Would Megan and Luke need even bigger houses just to keep their great-grandmother's serving platters, their grandmother's eggbeater, and my baskets from Botswana?

We had too much of everything but patience. Throughout the summer, we got sporadic messages from the bank through the seller's paralegal. First they wanted multiple estimates for every problem identified by the inspection; then they said never mind. We got a message telling us to apply for a mortgage, which meant gathering up many documents quickly; then we had to wait several more months, so our mortgage rate expired. We were told we'd be able to move in August, before school started. Then, with our house half packed, we were told to wait some more. Over months of waiting, several boxes got ripped open because someone needed a sweater or a roll of duct tape, while many sat undisturbed because we really didn't miss those books or puzzles when they were out of sight.

It didn't feel like way was opening with this house, but we had already signed a contract and made a deposit. Were we meant to back out of the deal, or just hang in there? I asked myself repeatedly. When I quit my canvass director job at age thirty and moved to Pendle Hill, I'd had clarity about what I was meant to do and confidence that some greater spiritual force was looking out for me. Same when I later moved to the mountains to write. Now, I felt more anxious than I had back when I'd had much less money to fall back on. Plus, pundits were predicting a "double dip" recession if Congress didn't reach an agreement on the US debt ceiling soon. I questioned the wisdom of trading our paid-off mortgage for a bigger house and new debt, but neither Tom nor I felt clear that we should change course.

After two more months of living out of boxes, when we were just about ready to give up on the house, the bank called and asked if we could settle the next week, in late October. It was anticlimactic, but we took it. The afternoon after closing, I let myself in to our new home and tried to figure out how to disable the dysfunctional alarm system, which beeped sporadically. Since it was Tom's birthday, I thought it would be fun to celebrate in our new dining room, so I set up an old card table and threw a blue tablecloth over it. I hung green and orange balloons and streamers from the crystal chandelier, and then ordered pizza. It was the best I could manage given the long list of things we needed to do before we could move.

With a short sale, we hadn't been able to ask the sellers to fix any-thing in the long-empty house, though we had gotten a reduction in the price to compensate for some of the needed projects. I was grateful for the friends who, over the next several weeks, hauled boxes and helped me clean, one wiping a layer of grime off the tops of the white kitchen cabinets, another scrubbing the discolored basement toilet. Still, we needed several professionals. The team I had originally scheduled to gut our mold-filled basement in August was now booked several weeks out because so many people had mold in the wake of Hurricane Irene. I scheduled a chimney guy to come fix an issue with the flue and some-one else to extend the radon pipe so it wasn't spewing under Luke's room. We knew from the inspection that two radiators weren't work-ing, but instead of the simple problem one contractor had suspected, it was a $4,000 problem that involved breaking open the plaster walls on the first and second floors.

While we were writing big checks, we decided to get an energy audit. We'd done it at our old row home and had gotten our heating bills lower than anyone else I knew in Philadelphia, about $50 max during January. I knew people with homes the size of our new one who paid up to $600 a month in winter, and that was not a club I cared to join. So, in came the energy auditor with a big machine that measured air leakage. His long report told us what we basically knew already: we had an old house that, while not the worst of its type, was far from being energy efficient. His "best bang for your buck" recommendation was to spray foam insulation along the base of the house and the third floor ceiling, which would earn us a $50 rebate from them, a $500 green tax credit, and reduce our heating bills for decades to come.

Unfortunately, the contractor discovered that the entire third floor had old knob and tube electrical wiring, a possibility that was hinted at in the inspection, but not made explicit. Turns out you can't spray foam insulation over knob and tube without it becoming a fire hazard, so with the third floor stripped to the bones and an already-tight schedule, we started calling electricians. Money was leaving our checking account at a pace I'd never seen before, and I felt how easy it would be to blow the inheritance my mother had saved a penny at a time.

The plaster dust gave me headaches, as did the constant negotiating with Tom. He usually wanted to go with the cheaper option, while I argued that sometimes paying more up front was cheaper in the long run, such as replacing the knob and tube wiring on the second floor when there were already holes in the walls from the plumber. Although always ready to pitch in when he was home, Tom's job made him less available, and I resented how much of my time was being sucked up by endless discussions with the parade of workmen: Chad, Chuck, Rick, Mike, Matt, Paul, Tom, and two Daves. Between the house projects, end-of-term grading, and spearheading a school fundraiser, I wasn't writing at all.

It didn't help that I kept hearing about couples who broke up after buying a bigger house. I didn't think we were in danger of that, but there was definitely more to argue about. One afternoon Tom and Luke primed my office, which would have made me extremely grateful except that they used the wrong kind of paint and then left little drips of white on the walnut floors, which made me apoplectic. Another day, Tom got mad at me for hiring a painter for the kids' third-floor rooms, which he thought we should do ourselves, though I didn't see how we had time before our scheduled move a few days later. He thought I was getting to be a spendthrift and was angry that I'd made the decision without him when we usually consulted each other about expenses.

Finally, one day in December, the movers arrived to get the big pieces of furniture we hadn't been able to shuttle to the new house in the back of our Camry. While the head mover went over the paperwork, we sent Luke to sit in the car with our high-strung dog, Spud, a pit mix we'd rescued from the pound. After several minutes, Luke phoned from the car to ask if we had forgotten about him, which we had. It seemed Spud, who was excited by all the commotion, had started farting in the car, increasing Luke's anxiety about being left there.

When we got to the new house, Megan, Luke, and I brought Spud through the living room and enclosed porch to the fenced yard where he raced and raced in circles around the twenty-foot-high rhododendron. He'd never had a yard of his own before, and we laughed at how happy he seemed to be off the leash. Luke egged him on, throwing something or pretending to every time Spud looked like he was going to stop. The kids sat on the porch with the panting dog and watched through the glass as the movers brought our piano and couch into the living room, along with the decorated Christmas tree that they'd put on the back of the truck. The three of them, at least, looked happy.

To me, life in the new house felt strange. After dinner, Megan and Luke headed up to their spacious third-floor bedrooms. With piles of homework and a bathroom of their own, they often didn't come down again until breakfast. Once the dishwasher was loaded and the food put away, Tom pulled out his laptop on the leather living room couch and started recording the dying people he'd visited that day, a chore that took even longer than it had when he used to do it on paper, though the computer was supposed to make it faster. With everyone else on an electronic device, I headed up to my newly painted office to have a good cry.

I missed walking by Megan's open door on the way to the bathroom and poking my head in casually. Now I had to trudge up to the third floor just to say hi. I missed Annie and Will—the best neighbors I'd had since Mmadithapelo—though they were moving soon, too. The couple that lived next door nodded hello as they walked their Dalmatian, but they seemed unlikely to pop by to borrow an egg anytime soon.

I'd felt unsettled for months, though I'd hoped that would fade once we finally moved. So far, it hadn't. Neither had the vague headache that I blamed on the plaster dust, which lingered no matter how many times I mopped the floors. Friends asked cheerfully, "How do you like the new house?" and it felt like a huge faux pas to admit the truth, that this moment of material abundance had left me feeling empty and alone.

Chapter Seven:
Lost and Counterfeit

*When change-winds swirl through our lives, especially at midlife,
they often call us to undertake a new passage of the spiritual
journey: that of confronting the lost and counterfeit places within
us and releasing our deeper, innermost self—our true self.*
—Sue Monk Kidd

I hired two young men from Bhutan to help me clear out our over-grown yard: Dilli and Devi, Hindus who had grown up as refugees in Nepal and now had a business doing odd jobs in Philadelphia. As we pulled the English ivy off the screens of the enclosed porch, Dilli fixated on the size of our house.

"How many people live in here?" he asked.

"Four," I said self-consciously.

He shook his head. "This house is too big." He said it about four times.

I remembered Botswana where people confused the phrases "very big" and "too big" since there was no such distinction in Setswana. I wondered if the same was true in Dilli's native language. Was he intending to criticize, or just making an observation? He was very sweet and didn't seem resentful, just honest about his reaction.

"In Nepal, how many people would live in a house the size of ours?" I asked as I drove them home.

"Fifteen," he said.

Dilli's reaction to our house only intensified my sense that, at forty-nine years old, my life was out of sync with my values. I thought of myself as a Quaker who had never cared about makeup and appearance, yet I had a $200 chemical peel scheduled at the recommendation of my dermatologist. A grassroots activist in my twenties who had campaigned on both environmental and economic justice issues, it had been some time since I'd protested anything or even had a bumper sticker on my car.

Soon after my conversation with Dilli, I was packing up some financial papers and became curious about one of the stocks we owned. It only took a quick Internet search to realize that the company specialized in hydraulic fracturing, a relatively new and controversial way to extract natural gas so deep it had previously stayed in the ground. I knew "fracking," as it was commonly called, was well underway in the Endless Mountains region where I had lived while writing my first book. The friends who owned the farm where Tom and I had gotten married, Larry and Laurie, had told us that gas companies had been quietly buying up leases for years.

I had good friends in the town of Dimock, where tap water full of methane had actually exploded a few years earlier, making national news and sparking debate about the health risks of fracking. It was with a little shock of horror that I realized that one of the companies drilling in Dimock was our most profitable investment.

To compound my growing unease with our lifestyle, I got a call from Mmadithapelo a few days after learning about the fracking stock. Knowing it was summer in the Southern Hemisphere, I asked if it was hot.

"Oh my God!" she said. "It is 45 degrees!"

Celsius temperatures always felt unreal to me, like Monopoly money, though 45 degrees did sound high. When I got off the phone, I googled temperature conversion and entered 45°C. The Fahrenheit box said 113°F. My mouth dropped open. "Holy shit," I said out loud.

One website said that because of climate change, it was so hot in Botswana that rain evaporated before it could be absorbed by the arid soil. I had wondered how Botswana was coping with climate change when I read the book *Hot* eleven months earlier. I had realized that it was unfair that people who did the least to create climate change were likely to face its worst effects and had taken note when Greenpeace International appointed its first African executive director, my friend from graduate school, Kumi Naidoo, whose experience was primarily in human rights and anti-poverty work. Now, hearing Mmadithapelo's firsthand report of the scorching heat, the connection between climate change and human rights suddenly felt more clear.

I opened Google Earth and entered Bobonong, now so sprawling I had to scroll around for several minutes before I located my old school. I zoomed in and moved slowly northward until I found the nearest river. The dry meandering sand looked almost white. Of course, the rivers in Botswana were often dry, I reminded myself, and the satellite image probably wasn't taken during the rainy season. I recalled how dependent farmers were on the scarce, seasonal rains, and how frequently people had talked about the weather and had mentioned it in letters. I remembered how the precolonial Batswana redistributed grain through their mothers in order to protect against drought and how that system had broken down under colonialism. I thought of Mmadithapelo's children, a daughter and son who were a few years older than my own. I thought of my former students—who threw me blankets on a chilly truck ride and who laughed because Americans kept gerbils as pets—and wondered how many of them were dependent on subsistence agriculture.

Then I remembered my own ancestors, those who died from the Great Hunger and those who fled from it, and I remembered my mother's bitterness toward the English more than a hundred years later. The predictions for famine in Africa were much, much worse.

So, at 3:00 a.m. I stared at the ceiling, tears streaming down my face, as Tom slept next to me under the down comforter. I looked in the dark at our ceiling fan, larger and classier looking than the one in our old house, and I wondered: How the hell did I become a woman who has a big house, a chemical peel appointment, and stock in a fracking company? How did I become so sucked into the American mainstream, and what can I do to create the kind of life—the kind of world—I really want?

A few days later, I showed up to the monthly meeting of Earth Quaker Action Team, the group that had sung "Where Have All the Flowers Gone" at the Philadelphia Flower Show. When I joined the room of about thirty people, I received warm hugs from those I recognized, including Walter Hjelt Sullivan, who had told me to meet them at the PNC pavilion, and Ingrid Lakey, whom I'd met at a Pendle Hill workshop a few years earlier. George Lakey, Ingrid's father, slipped in as the meeting began with stories from an action the week before that was part of their campaign to get PNC Bank to stop financing companies engaged in mountaintop removal coal mining.

Wanting to illustrate what they were for as well as what they were against, EQAT members had constructed two ten-foot white, cardboard windmills in a downtown PNC Bank lobby. Like at the flower show, the group had clearly commanded the space, singing songs, this time in green "Earth Quaker Action Team" T-shirts. While the police had not arrested anyone at the flower show, this time they had. When the police had issued their first warning, most of the group had moved outside to the sidewalk while the five willing to risk arrest remained singing in the lobby. After three warnings, the "Windmill Five" were handcuffed and put into Philadelphia police vans, while the Earth Quakers outside sang and cheered them. Now those who had been arrested took turns telling their stories to the larger group.

The youngest was a Bryn Mawr undergrad, the oldest a man in his seventies, who from the sound of it had a rap sheet longer than his grey ponytail. For some, it was their first arrest and an education in the realities of the criminal justice system. The scariest part, it seemed, was when they were separated. One woman with a health concern was sent to a different facility, where she had heard fights were common. Sitting alone in the police van, she had thought about the early Quakers, Martin Luther King, Jr., and Gandhi, and their examples had strengthened her through the night. In the early morning hours, she felt relief when she saw familiar green T-shirts pass her cell, and she didn't feel so vulnerable or alone.

Walter explained how he and the jail support team had called the families of those arrested, then stayed up to greet each person with food and a ride home as they were released at various times from the middle of the night till sometime the next morning. I was impressed with the thought that had obviously gone into deciding who would risk arrest and who wouldn't, and the appreciation that people offered each other, whatever their role. Hearing their stories was both inspiring and intimidating. I wasn't sure if I could really see myself spending a night in a Philadelphia jail, but when someone announced that EQAT would be singing Christmas carols with funny lyrics about mountain-top removal at a downtown PNC, I could imagine doing something like that.

After a full agenda, Ingrid announced that they were creating a new twenty-hour-a-week position, encouraging Quakers to "green" their money by withdrawing it from PNC Bank. I sat up in my chair as she described the job, which would use at least two of my skills: writing and understanding Quakers, who have a quirky, communal decision-making process. Maybe this job was the thing I'd been groping around for, I thought, the thing that would help me combat climate change and live more in sync with my values. When the meeting broke after a rousing song, I beelined for Ingrid, a redhead a few years younger than I am and a few inches taller. I asked for one of the few copies she had of the job description.

"Really?" she said, momentarily taken aback. "I didn't expect you to be interested in this sort of thing." She only missed half a beat before adding, "It's great you want to apply!"

Maybe it was because Ingrid knew of me as a spiritual writer and teacher, I thought, but still—what does it say about the way I'm living my life if Ingrid Lakey is surprised I'd be interested in work like this?

My enthusiasm for the position was only slightly dampened when I learned that Walter was also applying for it. Walter had risked arrest at the flower show and had stayed up all night supporting those who had gotten arrested at the windmill action. He had proven his dedication to EQAT. He also had plenty of experience working with Quakers—as the former dean of Pendle Hill and former codirector of a West Coast Quaker retreat center—so it seemed likely that Walter would be hired. Still, the excitement I felt every time I read over the job description prompted me to at least go through the application process.

In the wake of moving chaos, with boxes everywhere and Megan and Luke home on winter break, I sat down with my laptop and pulled up my old résumés. The most recent ones highlighted my publications and university teaching. The older ones included my canvass director job and the project proposal on social issues I had developed for Pendle Hill in the early nineties. It was fun reading through past accomplishments, cutting and pasting relevant bits into a new two-page document, trying to make my life sound like a coherent whole.

My energy had been scattered, I realized. When I listed it all out—volunteering (in my congregation, my precinct, my community garden, and at my kids' schools) plus teaching (at the University of the Arts and in recent years at Pendle Hill)—it was no wonder I'd only published two books. When you added in parenting and caring for my mother, it was a wonder I'd published anything, come to think of it. I knew I had the skills needed for the EQAT job, but much of my relevant experience was as a volunteer. Unlike Walter, who was only a few years older, I had never been a dean or director of anything. At age forty-nine, I realized with dismay, I had never really channeled my energy in one direction.

This was part of the reason I'd been getting increasingly tired of part-time university teaching, which felt like a side project rather than a career. I'd fallen into it eleven years earlier because the schedule enabled me to write and care for young children. I'd been feeling more resentful lately of our low pay, which was so pitiful some adjuncts taught at three or four different colleges just to get by. Even with only one class per term and subjects I enjoyed, like South African history, I was losing enthusiasm for grading papers and sending deficiency notices to the students who cut class, burdens I didn't have to deal with when teaching at Pendle Hill each winter.

As I polished my résumé for the EQAT job, I remembered an incident a few weeks earlier near the end of fall term, just before we moved. My undergraduate students had been researching South African artists, which had prompted a class discussion about meaningful work. One of the young men had looked at me and asked point blank, "Do you love what you're doing?"

"Yes," I said, though as I heard myself say it I'd realized that it was no longer true.

Standing in front of the class in my silk print blouse and my practical black shoes, I didn't have the nerve to correct myself on the spot, but I'd noticed how uncomfortable I felt about my answer. Now, as I pressed "send" on the EQAT application, I felt certain that it was time to move on, whether I got the job or not. When I told Tom that I felt ready to stop university teaching so I could work more on climate change, he shrugged and said, "You might as well do what you're called to do. You weren't making much money teaching anyway."

I would have felt bad backing out of my spring course at the last minute, but I had a hunch that my friend Amanda Kemp, who was qualified to teach it, might be interested. So I gave her a call over the winter break and said that I'd like to quit my teaching job if I could find a replacement.

"Funny, I was just thinking that I'd like to get back to teaching," she said.

I wrote a letter to the Liberal Arts dean resigning and recommending Amanda, who got the job without anyone else being interviewed. Being able to pass off my spring course so easily felt like an example of that Quaker concept of way opening, confirming my sense that it was the right thing to do, no matter what happened with the EQAT job. I went down to the university one more time to empty out my mailbox and say goodbye to the dean and his assistant, who after eleven years waved me off without fanfare. Riding the elevator down to the street and saying goodbye to the guards at the front desk, I noticed that my eyes were dry.

My interview with Earth Quaker Action Team was at the West Philly home of Carolyn McCoy, the clerk (or chair) of the board. West Philly was the neighborhood where my immigrant grandparents had started their family before moving to the suburbs. Now it had a health food co-op, a credit union, and signs like "No Fracking" and "War Is Not the Answer" in the windows. It was also home to several EQAT leaders. Carolyn, Ingrid, and Kaz Uyehara met with me around Carolyn's wooden dining room table. Over cups of steaming tea, we laughed about the way I had met up with the group at the flower show and how I had jumped right in, handing out flyers.

"You know some Quakers are saying that we are too confrontational," said Ingrid seriously. "They think it isn't 'Quakerly' to disrupt something like the flower show. What would you say to that?"

I laughed, thinking immediately of the early Quakers, who—convinced that the church of their day was not following God—would stand up in the middle of a church service and preach over the priest or minister, intending to disrupt religion as usual. Thousands of early

Friends were thrown in jail for their witness, including our most famous founder George Fox.

"I'd say, 'Have you read George Fox?'"

Ingrid chuckled but seemed surprised by my answer. "Fox directly challenged the authorities of his day in ways that would seem shocking to many Quakers today," I explained. "We've forgotten our history."

We talked about Earth Quaker Action Team's philosophy of non-violent direct action. Although I had first encountered the group when some of them were risking arrest, civil disobedience was only a small part of their strategy. They had also met with PNC officials to urge them to change their investment policy and had joined in bigger events organized by allied groups from Appalachia. EQAT had recently decided to launch a new initiative to get people to move their money out of PNC Bank until it stopped financing mountaintop removal coal mining companies. Carolyn said they wanted the person to start in early January, and for the first time during the interview I felt my chest tighten.

"Early January would be difficult, but if that's what you need, I can make it work," I said with less than total confidence. After a pause I added, "If you end up needing more than twenty hours in a week, Walter would probably be in a better position to do that."

Afterwards when I was honest with myself, I realized that even twenty hours a week would be a challenge. Megan could walk to her new high school, and Luke could take the public bus to middle school, but there were still soccer games and food shopping, not to mention teaching at Pendle Hill and the fundraising I had agreed to coordinate for the seventh-grade trip to Costa Rica. We were still emptying out our old house, which had to be spruced up before it was put on the market, and now I had more bathrooms to clean in the new house. I had wanted to write about issues related to climate change, but I hadn't even started a new Word document since "The Blessings of a Small House," which felt absurdly out of date. It was hard to imagine how I'd ever write much of anything if I got the EQAT job.

One day as I was driving a few more boxes from the old house to the new, the realization dawned that I'd be relieved if I didn't get the position. Just applying had helped me out of the part-time teaching rut and had made me realize that I wanted to focus my energy, but it didn't quite feel like the right thing at the right time. I exhaled with a little relief.

Two days later, I pulled my car over to take the call from Carolyn, who phoned to say that the position was going to Walter. She affirmed what a strong candidate I'd been and how they hoped I'd still get involved with EQAT. I thanked her and shared my sense that it might not have been the right time for me to take on a new job anyway, but that I really liked the organization and hoped to keep attending meetings. A few hours later, I called Walter to offer my congratulations, and we had a nice chat, affirming how much we respected each other and wishing each other well.

Near the end of the conversation, Walter said, "You will find the place where you can use your gifts, Eileen, because you have really amazing gifts." I was gracious and grateful, but when Tom came home from work and I tried to tell him what Walter had said, I couldn't get the words out because I was sobbing so hard.

I slid down to the hardwood floor next to the gas stove where I was cooking bowties for dinner as Tom peered over the granite counter concerned. In a few weeks I'd be teaching a Pendle Hill class called "Discerning Our Calls," where I would talk about identifying and using your gifts, though I had a piercing feeling that I wasn't fully using my own. In truth, I wasn't sure how I would even begin to teach a class about listening for and following divine guidance this year. In my twenties, I had felt connected to some spiritual force that was greater than myself when I looked out on a mountain range or up at a night sky. In my thirties, I'd often felt guided by that force and had many experiences of way opening. Now, in my late forties, I felt like I was slogging my way through life, talking about spirituality more often than I experienced it.

The next day, I met my friend Deb, and we walked along the Wissahickon Creek under the leafless ash and maple, stopping occasionally to appreciate a ray of sun coming through the wintry branches. Recently her husband Dave had been diagnosed with a brain tumor. In addition to the terrible shock, she was dealing with MRIs and neurologist appointments, as well as two kids and an unfinished dissertation. My struggles felt petty compared to hers, but I knew she also yearned to have a life that mattered, so I told her the story of the EQAT job, still relieved that I didn't get it, but still crying when I repeated what Walter had said to me.

"That's where God is," said Deb. "God's in that thing about wanting to use your gifts."

Driving in the car one day, I asked Tom what he thought my greatest gift was. After a pause he said, "Being able to see and articulate the connections between things."

I liked the sound of that, and it felt true. Both my academic degrees had been interdisciplinary, and most of my academic writing had been about connecting issues, especially those in different parts of the world. When people told me that my spiritual writing had helped them, it was often because it made them see the connection between some everyday dilemma they were facing and a larger spiritual principle. When I was running a meeting, I could often find the connection between different points of view and integrate diverse perspectives. If Tom was right and my greatest gift had to do with articulating connections, this moment of global climate crisis might be a time when that gift was particularly needed.

Talking to Tom or Deb often helped me clarify what I was thinking, the way journal writing did. The next week on our walk in the woods, I blurted out to Deb that I wanted to try to live more simply and to write about the connection between consumption and climate change, even though both seemed like contradictions just a few weeks after moving into a bigger house. Again I cried as I said it. Again Deb listened with compassion. She affirmed my intent, but added that she thought my hormones were out of whack.

"I'm usually the one who cries a lot," she observed. "This is not normal behavior for you."

She was right, and I instantly suspected the source of the problem. After years on birth control pills, I had quit around Thanksgiving at the age of forty-nine, and the crying had started a few weeks later when we were in the midst of house renovations and moving stress. I felt foolish that I hadn't connected my tears to hormones before.

Our culture is full of disparaging jokes about hormonal women, but in my experience, those times when the chemicals in my brain make me feel slightly out of whack are often gifts. Being raised by an exceptionally no-nonsense Irish woman taught me to suppress my feelings, and I sometimes needed a little help figuring out what lurked below my well-adjusted exterior. By jiggling loose my protective shield, a little PMS had sometimes helped me realize that there was something bothering me that I needed to address. Similarly, my recent hormonal storm had woken me up to the feeling that my life was out of sync and that I wasn't fully using my gifts. It hadn't made me feel things that weren't real; it was helping me become aware of feelings that were.

Still, it wasn't that pleasant, especially for Tom, who had been quietly wrapping his arms around me on the nights I couldn't sleep. I called a friend from college who was a gynecologist and asked her what to do.

"Eileen, go back on the pill," she said firmly, explaining that a woman's estrogen declines gradually through her forties, but at forty-nine mine had plummeted when I quit the pill abruptly. Even if I didn't want long-term hormone replacement, I could at least use it to taper off more gradually, she said, advising me to speak to my doctor at my next appointment.

I started a new package of pills, and within two days I felt my emotional equilibrium return. The 3:00 a.m. weeping stopped, though I still cried more than usual, aware of the currents churning under the surface.

The Sunday before Martin Luther King Jr. Day, I sat in a silent Quaker meeting for worship, watching the logs shift and crackle in the roaring fireplace in front of me. The next day in this room there would be a celebration of King's life before students and their families headed off to a day of service projects, from making crepe paper flowers for old people to collecting clothes for the poor. It had always annoyed me that King's legacy got reduced to "service," when his life had really been about challenging injustice with faith and love. He had articulated the connection between racism, materialism, and militarism. Today, I thought, we still needed to make those connections only with the added element of environmental destruction.

I felt my heart beating faster, a common sign that I was meant to stand up and speak, which anyone could do in a Quaker meeting when they felt moved by the Spirit. I rose off of the old benches and spoke into the silence about how the core Quaker values of simplicity, equality, and peace were all threatened by climate change, which would disproportionately hurt poor people and people of color, even though it was not their consumption that had done the most to fuel it. I mentioned that rising temperatures and famine were increasing violent conflict over food and water, especially in Africa. I also talked about love and how service was most useful when it gave people the opportunity to meet and love those who were different from them, which had been the greatest gift of my Peace Corps experience.

"Climate change in Africa is not just some abstract issue for me because there are Africans whom I love," I said, my voice cracking as I spoke.

Afterward two women came up to me—one black, one white—to say that my message had changed the way they thought about climate change.

Although I could finally sleep through the night, it felt like, in some deeper way, I had finally woken up.

Chapter Eight:
The Achilles' Heel of
Consumer Society

*The Achilles' heel of consumer society is that
it hasn't made us as happy as it promised it would. . . .
We've pursued the American Dream to no real apparent end.*
—Bill McKibben

L eaving the university gave me a little more mental space, a clut-
tered mind being one of the things that had made writing difficult. With the house projects mostly completed, the moving
boxes mostly emptied, and a few weeks before my winter Pendle Hill
course began, I started writing down my reflections on what had made
living simply in the United States so difficult.

To my surprise, I found part of the answer in *The Feminine Mystique*,
which I stumbled upon one day in the sunlit Pendle Hill library as I was
preparing for my course. I'd never actually read the feminist classic, but
flipping through the preface, I noticed it was finished a month before I
was born, nearly fifty years earlier. Out of curiosity, I checked it out for
winter bedtime reading. In a culture that glorified consumerism as the
path to a woman's fulfillment, Betty Friedan described:

> A strange stirring, a sense of dissatisfaction, a yearning that
> women suffered in the middle of the twentieth century in
> the United States. Each suburban housewife struggled with it

alone. As she made the beds, shopped for groceries, matched slipcover material, ate peanut butter sandwiches with her children, chauffeured Cub Scouts and Brownies, lay beside her husband at night—she was afraid to ask even of herself the silent question—"Is this all?"

Half a century later, I was shocked to recognize myself in this description.

I'd done more than chauffeur for the past fifteen years, didn't live in the suburbs, and didn't even have slipcovers, but I still felt a surprising kinship with the affluent women of my mother's generation. I was struck that, in example after example, they listed three things together: husband, children, and home—as if a woman expected her life to be perfect once she'd acquired all three. Although I loved my husband and children and had worked outside the home, I still related to the feeling that somehow I'd been hoodwinked, especially in terms of the house. Did I really think some extra bathrooms could make me feel fulfilled? Friedan argued that only using one's gifts could do that.

Friedan herself had been surprised to learn that at least some of women's dissatisfaction had been deliberately engineered. Almost accidentally, she'd met an advertising guru—like those in the show *Mad Men*, I imagined—who explained to her how companies could sell more products to women by manipulating their insecurities and deferred dreams. "The only way that the young housewife was supposed to express herself and not feel guilty about it was in buying products for the home and family," explained Friedan. Controlling 75 percent of purchasing power in the United States, she concluded, was a "ghastly gift" because it made women the targets of so much advertising.

Through in-depth interviews, the advertisers had discovered that they could sell the most stuff to women who stayed home with their children but who also had outside interests and didn't insist on doing everything themselves by hand or from scratch, the way my mother had. They wanted women who would appreciate the home washing machines that made my parents' laundry business obsolete, women who would buy mac and cheese mix and jarred pasta sauce. In other words, women like me. Again I felt a little shock of recognition, despite the five decades that had passed since Friedan's research.

I had wanted to be a writer and a stay-at-home mom, but I hadn't really been able to do both full time, so I'd made compromises. When my children were young, I had been adamant that macaroni and cheese should be made from scratch, preferably with hand grated organic cheese from a local and happy grass-fed cow. Somewhere along the way, I succumbed to the Kraft box with the little packet of orange powder that didn't look like it came from anything living. I had also enjoyed baking chocolate chip cookies from scratch, but when the kids wanted to bring something to school for their birthdays, I usually rushed by ShopRite for a few plastic boxes of cupcakes with brightly colored icing and sprinkles that looked like cardboard confetti. My frugal, health-conscious mother would be horrified on so many levels, though come to think of it, her generation didn't feel obligated to send a treat to school on birthdays.

Trying to balance writing and parenting, a lot of my ego had gotten wrapped up in being a "good mother," which, too often, I suspected, meant buying my kids the things they wanted. Wasn't that the American Dream, after all, that my immigrant grandparents came here, and my mother saved her nickels, all so I could give my children what none of us had ever had? Unexpectedly, a memory surfaced: the first time Megan cried, when we were still in the Scranton hospital. She was wailing so hard she couldn't latch onto my breast, so I'd instinctively held her close and sung the first lullaby that came to mind, inserting the word "Mama" instead of the traditional "Papa":

Hush, little baby, don't say a word,
Mama's gonna buy you a mockingbird.
And if that mockingbird won't sing,
Mama's gonna buy you a diamond ring. . . .

It was only now, reading Betty Freidan in our new house, that I questioned the significance of a song that teaches children to bury their feelings through consumption.

I'd been seeking simplicity since my return from the Peace Corps, but I had the growing sense that I hadn't been fully conscious of my choices. It wasn't so much the house and my chemical peel appointment making me uncomfortable, I realized, as the feeling that I wasn't who I thought I would be. Like Friedan, I wanted to figure out why.

As we touched up the paint in our old house to get it ready for market, I wondered what unseen forces had motivated us to go to all the trouble of moving when our old house seemed sufficient in hindsight. I knew my desire for an office and garden were real, as well as Tom's desire for "one quiet space." Although my children had said they were happy in the old house, I had still wanted them to have the privacy and space to entertain friends that I'd never had. Painting over the baseboards of Megan's old room, I found myself recalling one evening when I was in eleventh grade when students from my private high school stopped by our apartment, over thirty years earlier.

I'd been watching *The Love Boat* on the couch with my mother when the doorbell rang. Three classmates had seen a movie at the theatre downstairs, and the girl, who knew where I lived, had suggested they stop by to visit me. My mother buzzed them in, and I heard six feet stomping up our dark, narrow stairs. As they came down our apartment hall, past the one bedroom with no door, I heard one boy say with surprise, "She lives here?"

I felt betrayed by the girl, whom I'd thought was my friend, and judged by the boy, whom I barely knew. In fact, pretty much all I knew about him was that everyone talked about how long the driveway to his Main Line mansion was after he had a party to which I was not invited. Rightly or wrongly, I felt their visit was about seeing my apartment over the movie theatre rather than including me in their plans. I was tense and awkward. They did not stay long.

About ten years later, when I was in my twenties, I ran into that boy in a bike shop in Maryland. He was friendly and down-to-earth, and we chatted longer than we ever had in high school. As I walked back to my car, it hit me that I had misjudged him all those years ago when I assumed he was judging me. He may just have been surprised by the size of my apartment and may not have been the horrible snob I had assumed he was at the time. The baggage had been all mine, a realization that took me by surprise. Now at forty-nine, I wondered how much of our consumption—from the house to the Tamagotchis and confetti-sprinkled birthday cupcakes—had been motivated by a simple, unconscious desire to fit in.

When I looked around my house at the needless purchases I had bought for myself over the years, the greatest number were in the medicine cabinet, which was actually a whole closet. One shelf was reserved for items I'd used once: teeth whitener and concealer, purchased to make me feel more confident for my first televised author appearance; smelly jells to put on my hair, recommended by my hairstylist; Exotic Orchid lipstick that looked great in the glitter of the department store but garish at home.

I thought of women I loved and realized that we each negotiated beauty issues in our own way. For some, dying their hair felt important, a sign that they were not "giving up" on life or sexuality. For others, it was a bit of Exotic Orchid lipstick that gave them more confidence in the world. I had no problem with women making any range of choices—or men for that matter—and had made a range of choices myself at different times. It was the ceaseless advertising and pressure to conform to a certain image of womanhood that irked me.

Especially as the mother of a teenage daughter, I resented the way advertisers exploited the desire to fit in. I didn't try to stop her when Megan started using mascara, but I wanted to make sure she knew she was beautiful without it and that her appearance wasn't the measure of her value. I remembered Naomi Wolf's bestseller *The Beauty Myth* about exactly these issues, published in 1990. I googled more recent statistics and read that in a nine-month period, advertisers had spent $4.5 billion pushing personal care products like the ones I had bought and barely used.

When I was in my twenties, I didn't even shave my legs. Now, at forty-nine with a perimenopausal gut, I knew I was more susceptible to advertising messages about my appearance. With an Irish complexion and a family history of skin cancer, it seemed responsible to try to take care of my skin. But my dermatologist looked at my face the way a weary college professor scans another typo-filled paper, and it was sometimes hard to distinguish her medical advice from her marketing. Her office sold $50 facial cream, $35 sunscreen, and $150 laser treatments for Rosacea as well as chin whiskers, all of which she recommended for my poor face.

Shortly after buying the house, I'd finally heeded the dermatologist's advice and got a laser treatment for my rosacea, a common skin condition that makes many Irish people turn red and blotchy as they age. The worst cases, which were always featured on the brochures, developed big bulbous noses, like Jimmy Durante and Bill Clinton. I didn't want to look like Jimmy Durante or Bill Clinton, so I decided to give the treatment a try. The laser didn't hurt much, but it left me looking puffy and swollen for a few days. The technician said my skin was horribly dry, gave me samples of several expensive skin creams, and convinced me to get a peel two weeks before my second laser treatment.

Now—the afternoon before my chemical peel appointment, when I was in the midst of reading Betty Friedan and questioning my own consumption—I googled the process and felt sick at what I read on a medical website: "A chemical peel involves the application of toxic chemical solutions to the skin in a controlled manner, producing controlled tissue death." Why would I spend a few hundred dollars to have someone put toxic chemicals on my face to kill my skin? I asked myself. What had possessed me to agree to this? I called and cancelled, grateful that the receptionist did not ask why.

I felt lucky to do work that didn't demand perfect skin, Armani suits, or Prada pumps, though when I mentioned this to Deb on our next weekly walk, she pointed out that it wasn't just my profession that protected me from the pressure to project a certain image. Her husband Dave didn't have the luxury of not caring about his appearance because he was an African-American man. Wearing a nice suit changed how people perceived him, in his job as a university financial officer or even just walking down the street in Philadelphia. People's reasons for buying things, I realized, were often complicated. I didn't want to judge others, just be more aware myself.

Over our first weeks in the new house, we received a new catalog nearly every day—Pottery Barn, Raymour & Flanagan, Brookstone. I spent hours calling the toll-free numbers, asking to be taken off their lists. As I flipped through the glossy pages on the way to the recycling bin, I saw a world of calm and beauty, a world where nothing was out of place, and tasteful lamps illuminated scenes of elegance and ease. Even the dog crates were made of polished wood. It was hard to imagine the dogs that lived in them ever eating the pencils out of the kids' backpacks and then vomiting, as our mutt did, which made me wish we had a dog crate that nice. I had imagined a peaceful life in a bigger house, but we'd brought all our old problems with us, including a dog that vomited.

Although the previous owners of our house clearly liked to shop, they had left many of their things behind: boxes of now-moldy clothing, painted martini glasses, enough Christmas lights to decorate a city block, an expensive wine opener, a paper shredder, a leaf shredder, an unused digital picture frame, and a roasting pan that I later saw on sale at Bed Bath & Beyond for $99. I was thrilled to finally have a paper shredder and a leaf shredder, but after telling Deb that I wanted to live more simply, I felt a manic compulsion to get rid of the hand-painted martini glasses and the never-opened crème brûlée–making kit before Luke commandeered its small torch. I put the moldy clothes in the trash and sorted through the other things to see what someone else might want.

We really didn't need the three huge trash bags of colored Christmas lights, so I looked up Freecycle, a website where I'd heard people gave things away for free. A guy in Tucson, Arizona had founded it when— working for an organization that provided recycling services—he saw how much perfectly good stuff people discarded. Since reusing things is even better for the environment than recycling them, he drove around Tucson, trying to find good homes for things he'd salvaged. Soon he turned to e-mail and eventually the web. According to their website, thousands of regional Freecycle groups developed in eighty-five countries, saving five hundred tons a day from local landfills while building more generous communities.

Not only was there Freecycle in Philadelphia; there was a Yahoo group just for our northwest end of the city. I set up an account and posted my first message: "Offer: Three bags of colored Christmas lights." Even though it was two weeks after Christmas, we soon received an e-mail from a librarian whose former branch, in a low-income neighborhood, hadn't been able to decorate this year because of budget cuts. She wanted the lights for future years and arranged to pick them up the next night.

"Oh, thank you so much!" she gushed on my doorstep. "People will really appreciate these."

I felt lighter helping her carry the bags out to her car, despite the chill.

I couldn't imagine why our home's previous owners had held onto so much stuff when giving it away was so much fun. Come to think of it, I wondered, what made them buy it all to begin with? Why did these people buy crème-brûlée makers and digital picture frames that they never even took out of the box? And why did they leave it all behind? I was especially curious since these folks were underwater financially. They had neglected home maintenance and had resorted to a short sale, so clearly their resources weren't limitless. Yet there were thousands of dollars worth of things just abandoned. If it weren't for the absence of a bed, you might have thought they'd fled in advance of a hurricane.

Always glad to save money, I had been initially happy to see that the previous residents had left behind cleaning supplies, though I soon realized that I would never use so much cleaner if I lived to be a 105. There were eight cans of Comet, as well as several cans of Ajax, seven gallons of bleach, six different products for cleaning toilets, three different kinds of wood cleaner, an assortment of small bottles for cleaning specific surfaces such as brass or stainless steel, and enough hand sanitizer to kill all the germs in a five-block radius. I counted forty-four bottles of household cleaning products, a cornucopia of chemicals.

I remembered the advertising guru Betty Friedan had interviewed, who said that industry research indicated that women would be more enthused about housekeeping if it were made to seem as complicated as a profession through the marketing of specific products: "one product for washing clothes, a second for washing dishes, a third for walls, a fourth for floors, a fifth for venetian blinds, etc., rather than an all-purpose cleaner." The Mad Men had perfected their craft in the last fifty years, from the look of the stuff in our house.

In Botswana, I had used the same liquid soap to wash my dishes and my clothes. Frankly, it worked just fine for both. I hadn't owned any brass or stainless steel, so there was no issue there—a reminder that the less you have, the less stuff you need to take care of your stuff. Since returning to the United States, I'd expanded my variety of cleaners, using something different for the dishes, the laundry, the toilet, and the wood floors. Still, the staggering collection of cleaning supplies in my new house was intriguing to me. Did most Americans buy this many products, I mused? Or were my predecessors just addicted to Costco? Clearly they had a thing about germs.

I remembered a book I had read a few years earlier—*The Science of Fear: How the Culture of Fear Manipulates Your Brain*. Author Daniel

Gardner explained that advertisers often took a legitimate concern—like crime or germs—and just exaggerated the risks. One of his examples was the 1997 publicity for the hand sanitizer Purell, which aimed to move from its quiet niche market of medical professionals to a wider consumer market full of people who frequent germy places—public restrooms, subways, and libraries—basically everyone.

"Germs were a market waiting to be exploited," he explained. After a publicity campaign designed to make the whole world feel unsafe, there was an explosion of germ-fighting products, which Gardner described as "a gold rush."

I recalled Gardner's phrase, the "omnipresent marketing of fear," and his many examples of corporations intentionally whipping up public anxiety, from alarm and security fence salesmen to pharmaceutical reps. He argued that we were the safest society in human history, but also the most anxious, which rang true to me, remembering how anxious Americans seemed to me when I first came home from Africa.

Now that I was looking for it, I saw evidence of Gardner's thesis everywhere. One television commercial felt like a *Saturday Night Live* parody of fear mongering, except that it was so well produced. It began with an apocalyptic scene. Out of the grey rubble came a truck, which transported a man and his dog through a destroyed city until they met triumphantly with a few friends around a blazing fire. There was one guy missing, though. It turned out the men with Chevy pickups had survived, but their friend with the Ford didn't make it.

In the Chevy ad, the men who survived the apocalypse did so alone, aided only by an expensive product, though if there were ever truly an apocalypse, it would almost certainly be the people who worked together who would survive. In a postmodern city like my own, it was easy to imagine that we were all truly independent—driving our cars to the store when we needed an onion, instead of asking a neighbor—until something like a hurricane came along and people suddenly needed their neighbors to charge their cell phones, take a warm shower, or, God forbid, eat.

Participating in Freecycle felt like one little way to rebel against the Mad Men and the competitive consumption they encouraged. It modeled a way of being that felt more like my experience in Bobonong, where a person who didn't have a shovel could ask a neighbor. It was like an online village.

Tom found a trundle bed on Freecycle for one of his hospice patients, who had lost his job and become homeless when he became ill. Now the man was living with his wife on a cousin's porch. He had recovered enough to get kicked off hospice, thus losing his complimentary bed, though he still wasn't well enough to work. The Freecycle bed was the size of a single during the day, but thanks to a unique spring on the trundle, could pop up to create a full-sized bed for the couple at night. Tom recruited the man's mother-in-law, who had a minivan, to pick up the bed in an affluent neighborhood and deliver it to the low-income one where they were staying—a reminder that there were still people who had less than they needed only a few miles away from those who had too much.

I remembered the old Tswana practices that had increased food security—people helping in each other's fields and women redistributing grain through their mothers. It was fun to realize that a similar communal ethos could coexist and even be fostered by modern technology. I'd heard that some communities were setting up "time banks," where a person could give an hour of their time and skill and be repaid with an hour of someone else's time and skill. Philadelphia already had two car-sharing organizations. Instead of paying monthly car and insurance payments for a vehicle that was parked most of the day, you could join a collective with a fleet of cars parked across the city, electronic keys, and a website where you could reserve a vehicle when you needed one. Although it didn't seem economical for our family, for many people, paying only for the times when they actually drove was cheaper than car ownership.

Although saving money was one benefit of such arrangements, this movement was about more than that. Some groups used the term "Transition Town" because they hoped to transition away from our current system of ever-increasing consumption and reliance on fossil fuels, which didn't make people happy and made even less sense in the face of climate change. They believed that communities could increase their resilience and sow the seeds of a just alternative by fostering innovative models on the local level. It was an exciting idea.

I looked forward to giving away more stuff on Freecycle and to filling out my new garden with the irises and hosta people would post there come spring, but in terms of my time, I kept feeling a pull toward Earth Quaker Action Team and its mission "to build a just and sustainable economy through nonviolent direct action." EQAT's website described their founders as people who took short showers and often took the bus, but who realized that such measures were not enough as long as large institutions were exploiting people and the earth with no regard for the future. There was something about challenging the corporations that were profiting from the current system that especially spoke to me.

A few days after hearing that I didn't get the EQAT job, I got an e-mail from Ingrid, inviting me to join a few people who were thinking about how to upgrade the EQAT website to promote the new Move Your Money initiative. Having learned a lot about publicizing things on the web through my recent book promotion, it felt like another little way to share what I could. I joined Ingrid, Walter, and the organizer, Zack Hershman, in Ingrid's West Philly living room, and immediately felt at home chatting about EQAT's goals over a cup of Earl Grey tea.

It felt like a much more fulfilling use of my time than crying alone in my big house—or shopping for it, for that matter.

Chapter Nine:
The Invisible Shift

Frequently, as so many poets and psalmists and songwriters have said,
the invisible shift happens through the broken places.
—Anne Lamott

I continued to feel at peace with my departure from university teaching, even though I had not gotten the job that had initially prompted me to quit. I was happy to be writing more and enjoyed being involved with Earth Quaker Action Team. I hadn't had a moment's regret about cancelling the chemical peel appointment or giving away the stuff in the basement. But there were two decisions that still made me squirm: the fracking stock and the new house.

Honestly, I just hadn't been paying attention when we bought the stock. After my mother died, we found a financial advisor and told him we wanted to be "socially responsible" with the money I had inherited, but we didn't spend much time thinking through what we meant by that. Our advisor knew we were concerned about climate change, so on the theory that natural gas released less carbon than coal or oil, he had recommended stock in a company that produced natural gas. I hadn't asked many questions and had been content to see my statement balance rise.

In the past year, however, I had paid more attention to environmental news and had learned about the downsides. While it was true that natural gas itself burned cleaner than coal, it turned out that fracking—a relatively new method of extracting it—released methane, which was much worse for the climate than carbon dioxide. The process involved injecting water, sand, and an undisclosed chemical mix deep into the earth at high pressure in order to crack the shale to release the gas. Sometimes the chemicals leached. Though the companies claimed the process was safe, there were people living near fracking sites with headaches, dizziness, and rashes, not to mention fears of longer-term health problems.

The gas boom in places like Pennsylvania was making natural gas cheaper nationally—welcome news to most customers, though cheap gas also made alternatives like solar less profitable than they would be otherwise, arguably keeping our society dependent on fossil fuels. The fact that I somehow hadn't realized how our most lucrative stock was making those profits was just another sign that I hadn't been paying enough attention to my choices; now I was. Selling the stock wouldn't stop the company from fracking, but it would help move my life into closer alignment with my ideals. After discussing it with Tom, I made the call and cashed it out.

The house decision was more complex and harder to undo. The children were comfortably settled in their bigger rooms, and Tom was enjoying meditating in the guest room. It was even beginning to feel like home to me, now that most boxes were unpacked and I had found a shelf in the kitchen to display my Botswana baskets. Still, I bristled every time someone came to visit and said, "Oh, your house is so beautiful! You have so much more space. You must be so happy!" Deb assured me the house was only average by American standards, but I still remembered the pang of guilt I felt when Dilli told me that fifteen people would live in a house the size of ours in Nepal. Why should I feel guilty? I thought defensively. We had to live somewhere.

Lately I'd had a remarkable run of serendipity when it came to books, picking up a volume at the exact moment that I was musing on its subject. Continuing that pattern, I stumbled on a book that asserted that a common cultural characteristic of the Irish was "the experience of guilt associated with success and material goods." I felt another little shock of recognition. Although Hollister and Deb both assured me that the Irish did not have a monopoly on guilt, it was both humbling and reassuring to consider that my ambivalence toward the house might be part of some wider cultural pattern. I thought of my mother's brother, who died with $3,000,000 in savings and gaping holes in the bottom of his worn old shoes. There was an Irishman with issues about his own success, I thought.

Trained as a blacksmith by his immigrant father, my Uncle Joe had spent his career shoeing top thoroughbred racehorses, including one Triple Crown winner. To see his filthy work coat hanging off his lean frame, you'd never suspect his skill and strength. He never took a day's vacation in his life, until the age of seventy-six when he was kicked by a horse and needed twelve pins in his leg. After a six-month recovery, he returned to the track to work for seven more years, until the day he walked himself into the hospital with pneumonia and never walked out again. Always reluctant to spend money, he died with a dead battery in his hearing aid, two days before his Medicare nursing home benefit would have run out. I joked that he'd planned it that way.

According to my mother, Joe had been a miser since childhood, putting every nickel he earned in the bank as soon as possible so as not to lose interest, getting angry with his mother if he was forced to delay a deposit by even a day. For as long as I knew him, he lived in a greasy garage down by the Delaware River, which included a simple cot, a toilet, and mouse poop sprinkled among boxes of old horse-shoes. He put his earnings into tax-deferred annuities, which is how he accumulated the $3,000,000, though he never thought like a typical wealthy person. If he had, he might have invested in a tax attorney, who would have told him the disadvantage of putting all your money in tax-deferred annuities. As it happened, when he died, the federal, state, and city governments took well over half his money in taxes, prompting my Democratic husband to observe wryly, "It's enough to make you want to become a Republican."

Why would someone with $3,000,000 live in a garage full of mouse poop with holes in the bottom of his shoes and a dead battery in his hearing aid? I wondered. I couldn't help contrasting my uncle's Spartan life with the shopping fetish of our house's previous residents, though come to think of it both felt very different from the lifestyle I had enjoyed in Bobonong, where people found joy in simple things. Instead both Uncle Joe's austerity and the chemical-cleaner hoarding felt rooted in a scarcity mentality—a deep distrust that there would ever be enough. Even on his deathbed Uncle Joe wouldn't tell anyone where he'd put his safe deposit key, which was found hidden in a stack of paper towels in his garage.

I remembered my mother telling me that their older sister Mary had asked Joe for a loan in the 1950s in order to open a neighborhood bar with her husband. Joe refused the loan and then refused to speak to Mary for the next twenty years. Recalling this story, I suddenly connected it to another bit of Irish history I'd read—that during the Great Hunger, people sometimes cut themselves off from friends and relatives to circumvent the Irish cultural norm of sharing. How exactly had my mother's family survived the famine when half the people in County Cavan had not? I thought with a shudder. Did my great-great-grandmother Rose share food with her siblings or lock her door to protect her five children, eating in a windowless corner the way I hid in the corner of the school library in Bobonong when I received Girl Scout cookies in the mail and didn't want to share with the students?

If Irish culture had been traditionally rooted in interconnection and the idea that "People live in each other's shadows," then no wonder the Irish who had endured and ultimately prospered were wracked by guilt and a fear of losing what they had gained. While the *Keeping-Up-With-the-Kardashians* aspect of American culture encouraged people to enjoy and show off their wealth, even pretending that they had more than they actually did, my mother's family did the exact opposite, keeping such a tight grip on their cash that they seemed to go through life with their fists clenched.

My mother was less extreme than Uncle Joe in her frugality, but like him she never really enjoyed the money she had saved, keeping the same mattress for thirty years, even though the accumulated dust mites couldn't have been good for her lung condition. When I finally dragged her to Sleepy's mattress store a year before her death, she announced to the salesman upon arrival, "The last time I bought a mattress, Jimmy Carter was president." He didn't know what to say.

Until now I'd assumed I was of a different tribe. When I inherited my mother's money, I treated myself to a massage and then consulted a financial advisor. Since Tom and I hadn't saved much on our modest incomes, we had decided to save most of it for college and retirement, though we did significantly increase our charitable contributions, something my mother never did. I was the epitome of balance, I'd thought—not too extravagant, not too miserly. It was only now, a few weeks after crying in the middle of the night about my house with a laundry chute, that I began to wonder if I'd inherited the Irish "guilt associated with success and material goods" along with my stocks and bonds.

One day, when Tom and I were sitting at the table after dinner, I asked him if he thought there was anything useful about guilt. Tom had a master's of divinity and a master's of social work, not to mention a long history of working to help other people.

"Guilt is a sign that something is wrong," he said after a moment's thought. "It is valuable if it motivates you to do something to correct the problem, but if you feel guilty about something that you can't do anything about, then it's unhealthy." He pointed out that in his Roman Catholic tradition, guilt was supposed to lead to confession, reconciliation, and change. "If it just leads to feeling bad and helpless, then it's not useful."

Tom's distinction between things we could control and things we couldn't was helpful. In addition to whatever baggage came from my family history, I knew that the house had also come to symbolize my "carbon footprint," a very rough approximation of our annual individual contribution to climate change. In Philadelphia, it was impossible for me to live the way I had in Bobonong—with no heat or electricity, most destinations within walking distance, and meat that came from a cow shot a hundred yards from my house. No matter how noble, no Pennsylvanian was going to have a carbon footprint as low as someone living in a mud hut in Malawi or Mozambique, where the amount of carbon emitted to sustain the average person's lifestyle was one-thirtieth of the average American's.

Even so, we did have choices. The size of our house was within our control, obviously, as well as the temperature we set our thermostat, though we had no individual control over the process that produced the gas that heated our home. Similarly, we chose what kind of food to eat and where to buy it, but our options were shaped by farm policies that favored big agribusiness, which used a lot of fuel to produce and transport food. Given this tension, I wondered, how guilty should I feel about my carbon footprint, which was much lower than the US average, but much higher than the global average?

I raised this with Deb one day as we sat at her table after a walk. I knew that she struggled with guilt herself, as a person who felt called to work on issues of racial and economic inequality but who came from a white family that owned two vacation homes. We had joked about the fact that some of her ancestors were among the Protestant landown-ers in Ireland who'd exported food to England during the famine. I suspected she was even more prone to guilt than I was.

"As a twenty-year-old, in all my idealism, I believed I was going to solve the problems of the world, and I just couldn't," said Deb, recalling the years in her twenties when her Christian faith led her to live and work in a poor, violence-torn neighborhood. Although it was painful, she'd found it liberating to accept the limits of what she could do. She needed to do the best she could to live in sync with what she called her "convictions," without feeling guilty for things beyond her control. It was pretty much what Tom had said, and I nodded in agreement.

"I think people are sometimes afraid to be conscious because they are afraid that then they'll have to try to fix everything," Deb added. "But that's not necessarily what it means. Being conscious just means that I am willing to make a deliberate choice."

For example, she said that being my friend and listening to my dilemmas had made her more aware of the environmental effects of her own consumption, which hadn't been a big issue for her before. Now she tried to turn off the water when she brushed her teeth and turn off her car instead of letting it idle when she picked her boys up from school or baseball. Nevertheless, she couldn't do everything "right" all the time, especially when she was feeling weary and overwhelmed. So during this arduous period when she was finishing her dissertation and her husband Dave was still getting chemo for his brain tumor, she had consciously chosen to use paper plates for a few months to avoid doing dishes.

"I know it is bad for the environment as a habit," she said. "I know it is wasteful of my money and not something that I would feel com-fortable doing long term, but it is a conscious choice." She said that in moments when she fell short of her own standards she tried to give herself grace.

"Having a husband with a brain tumor while you're writing your dissertation is a really, really good reason to use paper plates," I interjected. "No way should you feel guilty about that!"

Deb said that she appreciated that I could try to live by my own convictions without trying to guilt-trip her, and that feeling no judgment from me had actually helped her to become more open to thinking about her environmental impact.

"I'm so glad to hear that," I said, "because I worry that as I become more committed to writing and speaking about simplicity I'm just going to become a finger-wagging guilt monger, and I don't want to be that person." After a moment's pause, I added, "Also, I don't think that actually works."

I told Deb the story of making a conscious choice to leave my travel mug at home when I was taking the train with Luke to a Quaker conference and the unpleasant encounter I'd had with the woman I'd nicknamed the Smug Mug Lady.

"I still don't know if she was trying to make me feel bad for using Styrofoam, or if she just triggered a reaction because I was feeling unable to live as simply as I wanted," I said, refilling my water glass.

Deb said that years before someone had told her that there was something called "false guilt," which could fester and become shame. "There are two pathways to that. One is that you get a conviction, and you ignore it, and so you end up in this bad place. But the other is that you buy into somebody else's shaming of you."

I recalled something I'd once heard about the difference between guilt and shame. "Someone said that guilt meant you felt bad about something you did, and shame meant you felt bad about who you were," I recounted. "The person said that shame didn't serve any life-giving purpose, but guilt did when it kept you from doing wrong or motivated you to make amends for your mistakes."

Deb nodded in agreement, pointing out that some people were especially prone to being shamed, especially if they had that in their past. "So there needs to be discernment about that," she said, adding that when you felt a true conviction about something, it was important that you acted on it, otherwise it could linger and make you feel horrible.

"It's learning to actually do the little thing when you feel that bit of conviction though you kind of want to ignore it because it seems like such a little thing that you don't know how it would matter." It was part of her spiritual path, she felt, to trust that those little nudges mattered.

I remembered two years earlier when I had tried eating just a little less every day—half a baked potato instead of a whole—and ten pounds had slid off easily. My original motivation had been to reduce my environmental impact, but I had comforted myself with a Starbucks hot chocolate after the weight-loss hypnotist mocked me. Now, I was feeling the impulse to try cutting down on my food consumption again. This time my resolve was stronger, partly because the action wasn't rooted in guilt but in a desire to be faithful to an inward nudge.

Food, transportation, and housing were the biggest contributors to our carbon footprint, and food seemed particularly symbolic of the whole consumption dilemma. Sumptuous advertising images and large portion sizes at restaurants encouraged us to eat more than we needed, airbrushed magazine images made us feel bad about our resulting obesity, and gyms and diet gurus profited from our shame. Meanwhile all that excess food production released carbon into the atmosphere, so eating too much was literally bad for me and bad for the world. I wouldn't starve myself, or anything. Just eat a little less, especially less meat, which took more energy to produce commercially than vegetarian food.

Whenever I'd tried to limit my food for solely vain reasons, it never worked. I ended up feeling deprived and pigging out worse than before. Even on the few occasions when I'd tried fasting as a spiritual practice, I seemed to gain weight because I ate so much after the fast to make up for my sense of deprivation—eating a basketful of jelly beans and chocolate bunnies after forty days of modest Lenten self-denial. Now, I paid more attention to what triggered my overeating. I noticed that a glass of wine at dinner reduced my self-control, so I cut back on wine as well as chocolate because sugar only made me crave more food. When we ate out, I brought a plastic container with me for leftovers, which my children found mortifying.

Even so, I ordered too much—or the servings were too large. It was hard to bring home a little salad, so more often than not I just finished what was on my plate. The idea of not wasting food was so deep in my

Irish blood that I just couldn't let the plate go back to the kitchen with food on it. I also found it hard to resist peer pressure. "Oh, come on. It's my birthday!" a friend said, and soon I had a glass of pinot grigio in one hand and a slice of German chocolate cake in the other.

At home it was a little easier. I set the globe on the windowsill opposite where I usually sat at dinner and turned it so that Africa was facing me, remembering the previous summer's famine in Somalia. I thought of my malnourished Irish ancestors and the landlords who lived in plenty, feeling now a little more compassion for them as I realized how afraid they must have been of the hungry hordes. After a few weeks of looking at the globe, I noticed that I was losing weight again, though I tried to remember that weight loss was an indicator that I was eating less, not the ultimate goal. Still, the fact that eating a little less would benefit me, too, was not insignificant.

When I was writing my first book, one of the women I interviewed said that there was a promise in the Christian commandments, "Love God first, and love your neighbor as yourself." She said the promise was that there were "choices that cut all ways"—ways of acting that honored God, self, and others. I had found this idea a refreshing alternative to the self-denial extolled by some traditional religions, on one end of the spectrum, or the self-indulgence promoted by some New Age teachers, on the other.

One of my favorite "choices that cut all ways" was going to a locally owned coffee shop that served fair-trade organic coffee and paid its workers well. They also gave their coffee grounds away for compost and had a recycling program that put Starbucks to shame. Unfortunately, they were kind of pricey, so Tom preferred Dunkin' Donuts. He would rather save on expenses and give more to charity, but I preferred the choice that gave me better-quality coffee and served the community simultaneously. To some, it might have looked like I was wasting money on my own pleasure, but I knew my local coffee shop also created a multicultural communal space that provided more than lattes. To paraphrase author E. B. White, I chose to believe that we could both save the world and savor it.

I started trying to savor my house, appreciating the dark wood floors and the grandeur of the two-story rhododendron outside our bedroom window. I'd remember Dilli's comment about our house being "too big" next time we moved, but since that was not likely to be soon, I'd look for opportunities to use our spacious living room for building community. Tom had already hosted a gathering of his small prayer group from church and had scheduled a meeting of a board he was on, a housing program for homeless men. I could host my writer's group, or maybe an EQAT meeting, I thought, if that were ever needed.

Looking out over the closed buds of the massive rhododendron as I sat on the bed where I had cried in despair only a few weeks earlier, I realized that one of the blessings of this house was the crisis it had sparked. My 3:00 a.m. discomfort had woken me up and made me want to live more faithfully, and though I knew I was not through the other side of it yet, my angst about my consumption had already led to several positive changes, including more writing time and less junk in the basement, not to mention my belly.

Deb affirmed the way I was starting to think about the house on our next walk in the woods. "It doesn't do anybody any good to just feel bad about what I have," she said reflecting on her own experience with privilege, "but then it becomes really important to be conscious about making sure I'm using what I have to do what I'm called to do in the world."

I agreed. Making sure I was doing what I was called to do was definitely the next step.

Chapter Ten:
The Place God Calls You To

*The place God calls you to is the place where your deep gladness
and the world's deep hunger meet.*
—Frederick Buechner

E ach winter I taught "Discerning Our Calls" at Pendle Hill, the spiritual study center where I had explored my own call to write almost twenty years earlier. The nine-week course focused on the process of listening inwardly, paying attention to outward signs about where our gifts were most needed, and sifting those influences to discern what we were called to do. The students often came with high expectations, many of them in life transition, impatient to figure out their futures.

And here was their teacher, still in the midst of her own rocky renewal, feeling distant from God, and not entirely over the crying. I had two consolations: first, Pendle Hill was the kind of place where people were very tolerant of weeping and might, in fact, see it as a sign that you were being spiritually deep, not just perimenopausal; second, I believe we teach what we need to learn, and this class seemed like it might be just the thing for me at the moment.

During the first class, people from their twenties to their seventies gathered in the Pendle Hill library on a mixture of soft couches and old wooden chairs. With morning light streaming through large windows, I explained that spiritual discernment—the process of seeking God's guidance—sometimes involved recovering a piece of ourselves that had gotten lost over the years. As an icebreaker, I asked each person to say their name and recall something they'd loved doing as a child. I shared how much I'd loved walking in the woods as a Girl Scout. As we moved around the circle—which included people from four continents—each person lit up recalling times spent in nature, jumping rope, making things with their hands, or singing, which turned out to be a common theme.

After coming home from the first class, I reached for my guitar and pressed my soft fingertips against the dusty strings as I tuned them. In Botswana I had played the guitar and sung at least a few times per week. Also when I lived at Pendle Hill as a student, come to think of it. Alone in my house, I heard my voice, tentative and tight from lack of use. I only made it through three songs before my uncallused fingers started to hurt.

I went up to my office closet and fished out a Rubbermaid box of old journals and started flipping through them, curious what other pieces of myself I had forgotten. There were a few colorful journals with Tiffany windows on the cover, which I'd bought as a student at the Pendle Hill bookstore almost twenty years earlier. When I gave up regular employment to write full time I turned to the cheaper black-and-white composition notebooks, which outnumbered the others in the pile. There was also the leather journal of my childhood. The first few pages were ripped out to hide some secret pain, though now I couldn't remember what it was. The ripped pages felt symbolic of the ways I had been taught to hide my feelings, the result being that I often didn't have access to them myself.

My mother used to say I was "too sensitive" whenever I cried. It was only when I came to Pendle Hill at age thirty that I felt encouraged to pay attention to my emotions and to let tears come when I was moved. It was there that I read Trappist monk Thomas Merton's liberating insight that stripping away the socially conditioned masks we use to hide our real feelings is an important part of spiritual growth. When I shared this during the third week of my Call class, it felt like a reminder to myself.

During the fourth class, I shared how deeply moved I had been by a performance of *Our Town*. In the final act of Thornton Wilder's famous play, the recently deceased female lead goes back in time to witness a day in her life—her twelfth birthday, an ordinary day. Her mother is rushing to prepare breakfast for her daughter's birthday, but not really paying attention to her. The dead daughter finds it unbearable to watch as she realizes that the living don't really appreciate how precious life is. Watching the scene in a darkened theatre, I had been overcome by the realization that I was just like that mother, rushing, not seeing or appreciating what was right in front of me, especially my family. When the house lights had come on at the end of the play, I was still mopping my eyes.

When I repeated the story to the Pendle Hill class, I got choked up again, which made me slightly embarrassed. After the two-and-a-half-hour class, I walked to the dining hall for lunch with one of the Friends in Residence, a role that is sort of like a village elder. Still thinking about my tears during class, I confided that I thought I was perimenopausal.

"Oh, that was a bad decade!" she said with sympathy. Then, seeing my horror at the word "decade," she added quickly, "But I feel terrific now that I'm in my sixties!"

After going through the lunch line and filling my plate with stir-fried vegetables and brown rice, I sat at a table of six older women. I gingerly mentioned my recent weepiness, and one said, "I got through menopause by watching *The Bridges of Madison County* thirty times," which made us all laugh so hard I wasn't the only one crying.

To counterbalance all the depressing books I'd been reading, I had recently picked up one with a funny title, *Marrying George Clooney: Confessions from a Midlife Crisis*. Amy Ferris's satirical and sometimes lurid memoir claimed that menopausal women everywhere were up at 3:00 a.m. googling their ex-boyfriends or fantasizing about what their lives would be like if they had married George Clooney instead of the guy snoring next to them. I laughed out loud when I read it because I had in fact been googling ex-boyfriends myself lately, but only in the daylight—which, I suspected, might be worse. I knew it was just a symptom of questioning my own life. Still, a nasty little part of me was pleased to see that the guy who had turned down my invitation to my high school prom had gained more weight than I had.

Along with making me weepier, my hormonal changes had brought out the crabbiness in me, which had at least helped me to recognize some resentment I'd been harboring. Luke's whole seventh-grade class would be going for ten days to Costa Rica. During eighth grade, several Costa Rican pen pals would come stay with our families for a few weeks. The program was a real cultural exchange, not just a fancy trip for privileged North Americans. It was the kind of opportunity I wanted for my children and the Costa Rican kids, so I'd volunteered to help with the fundraising but ended up in charge of the whole darn thing.

I'd felt snookered into a seemingly endless time commitment, my resentment exacerbated by the fact that most of the work was done by mothers, though many had jobs as demanding as the fathers. One was a nurse who worked the night shift and then came in to sell hot dogs every Friday on no sleep. There were lots of dads, including Tom, who showed up on the day of a big event and did whatever needed to be done—filling the dunk tank for the Fall Fair, hauling out trash bags afterwards, and rearranging tables in the lunchroom after the Costa Rican dinner. But it was mothers who bore the psychic load, who made the lists of what needed to be done, carrying the details in their heads, and sending scores of e-mails. The gender imbalance was pissing me off.

I'd snapped at the Spanish teacher (who was an old friend) when she e-mailed me the Costa Rica dinner invitation to proofread. We had just moved into the new house, and our phone and Internet weren't hooked up yet, so I had specifically asked to be left out of the proofreading. My overreaction had made me realize that something was out of balance in addition to my hormones. It felt too late to back out of the Costa Rica fundraising, so I counted the weeks until the elaborate sit-down dinner, the last major fundraiser of the year, was over.

My irritation with the fundraising made me more attentive to the gender imbalance at home. When the children were young, I consciously chose to be the primary caregiver, even though it meant putting my writing on the back burner. Now that the children were getting older and I was ready to work more, I noticed with frustration that I was still the one who felt responsible for remembering when the kids were due to see the dentist. I was the one who filled out the camp medical forms, signed the permission slips, picked up extra cans for the canned-food drive, RSVPed for the soccer team dinner, scheduled the teacher conference, renewed the auto insurance, stopped the mail for vacation, and remembered to get the dog his annual rabies shot and a bordetella vaccine before he went in the kennel. More than cooking or driving to soccer games, it was the psychic weight of so many details that felt onerous.

One evening when the kids had left the dinner table—after I'd let our toilet paper supply run down to the last roll just to see if Tom would notice—I told him that I felt I needed to make more mental space for whatever I was called to do around climate change. I took a deep breath and added, "It would really help me to do that if I didn't feel like I was the person who had to remember everything that needs to be done at home."

"I do a lot already," said Tom. "I walk Spud every day. I do the dishes every night. I cook on weekends." I could feel my chest tighten.

"I know you do a lot," I said trying to keep my voice steady. "I do a lot, too. But in addition to all the things we both do, I feel this mental weight from having to remember so much little stuff. Like buying more toilet paper or heartworm medicine for Spud or picking up the trash that I've noticed by our curb for two days that no one else has picked up yet." After a moment's pause I said tightly, "I just need you to help notice stuff like that."

After a long pause, Tom said, "Could you make me a list of things you'd like me to notice?"

I wanted to scream, but didn't.

I remembered several people I knew—friends and former students from the discernment class—who'd entered a period of rebirth only to find that their spouse or partner was threatened by the change. Sometimes the partner wanted the person to continue playing a certain role. Sometimes the partner found the other person's transformation threatening because they didn't want to have to think about changing themselves. Sometimes the relationship could not survive the strain. Remembering these stories made me appreciate Tom, who, although confused by my crying and my attempt to renegotiate chores, at least understood the urge I felt to use my gifts in meaningful work. I was pretty sure he'd stick with me through this, though I knew it wasn't easy on him.

In the fifth week of the Call class, we discussed the tricky business of discerning when to respond to other people's needs and requests. Sometimes people found their calling by doing what was asked of them, I said, like Martin Luther King, Jr., who was nominated to lead the Montgomery bus boycott, a job he probably wouldn't have volunteered for. There was something to be said for meeting the need in front of you. On the other hand, pleasing other people could pull you away from the work you really felt called to do. It was important to pay attention to whether the things you were encouraged to do—either by the people in your life or society at large—felt in sync with your gifts and inner guidance, I said.

As I continued reading my old journals, as well as some old letters I'd kept copies of, I was shocked to notice how much energy I had expended over the years worrying what other people thought of me, especially men. In one letter from Botswana to my college friend Maureen, I spent eleven pages speculating about whether or not some guy liked me—eleven, out of a fourteen-page letter from Africa! My forty-nine-year-old self wanted to go back in time and shake that girl. Even in my work life, I saw in my journals, I had worried how others would judge my performance as a canvass director or how I could design a social issues program for Pendle Hill that would make everyone happy, including those with diametrically opposed opinions about what it should be.

I was not totally beyond caring about other people's judgments, I realized. Recently I had felt misunderstood by two good friends, who seemed to take it personally when I tried to change the patterns of our friendship. When our children were toddlers, we had started sharing leisurely lunches, which were sanity savers during those years. As I'd grown in my commitment to my writing, however, I'd felt an escalating tension over the fact that I no longer wanted to take a three-hour lunch with a bottle of wine in the middle of a Tuesday, even if it was only every few months. If scheduling lunch had caused so much hurt, what would it cost to really reorient my life?

I remembered how painful it was to feel separate from an old friend when I came home from the Peace Corps and watched her leave the tap running. I thought of how hard I'd found it to say no to my children when they wanted some overpriced piece of plastic and how hard it was to say no to the Costa Rica fundraising, even though I hadn't wanted to do it from the start. I remembered the less-famous second part of the Great Law of the Iroquois: "We must consider the impact on the seventh generation . . . *even if it requires having skin as thick as the bark of a pine.*" My skin was more like the papery bark of a birch.

A week before the Costa Rica dinner, I attended a talk by Quaker activist and teacher Steve Chase, who was a Transition Town leader in his own New Hampshire community. He told the story of Martin Luther King, Jr.'s 1967 speech to the American Psychological Association. Facing a crowd full of people whose profession was designed to help people fit in and function in society, King had argued that it was actually pathological for a person to become well-adjusted to a dysfunctional society. King challenged psychologists to help ordinary citizens deepen their capacity for what he called "creative maladjustment." Speaking to a room of seventy Quakers who wanted to think about ways to lessen their own and their society's environmental impact, Chase challenged us to become maladjusted ourselves, to reject the norms of a culture that was destroying the earth and its people.

King's framing helped me to be less self-conscious about my little oddball choices. The night of the Costa Rican dinner, the school cafeteria was draped with strings of Christmas lights as a hundred guests sat at lunchroom tables transformed with tablecloths and floral centerpieces. The seventh graders were dressed as waiters as they served chips, salsa, and ceviche, made with fish and lime, followed by heaping plates of rice with chicken, shrimp, or vegetarian pasta. I knew that the portions during the sit-down meal were always enormous, so I'd brought a plastic container to save half my meal and avoid overeating. My children rolled their eyes at what an embarrassing weirdo their mother was, but I was determined to be maladjusted.

A week later, when I finished writing the last thank you notes to people who had made an extra donation to support the dinner, I put down the pen and exhaled. I felt done. *Done.* I had to give up this kind of deadening chore to make space for whatever work I was really called to do.

The next Tuesday in the "Discerning Our Calls" class, I wrote my favorite quote about discernment up on newsprint: "The place God calls you to is the place where your deep gladness and the world's deep hunger meet." It was by Frederick Buechner, a Presbyterian theologian known for encouraging people to find grace in their daily lives. I'd always loved the graceful balance at the root of this quote and the invitation to find the choices that cut all ways. Now I remembered my emotional reaction when Walter said that I'd find the place to use my gifts; using them in a way that met the world's deep hunger felt like a key to finding my own deep gladness.

Realizing we didn't need any more stuff, Tom and I had given each other retreat weekends for Christmas. I finally took mine in February in the Endless Mountains where Larry and Laurie had built a beautiful home with a wide porch overlooking a kidney-shaped pond. To the left was a grassy hill that led past the noisy chicken coop and their large enclosed garden to the spot where Tom and I had gotten married almost seventeen years earlier in front of another, smaller pond. I dumped my bags in the geodesic dome they kept for guests—slightly larger than my Bobonong rondavel, with a small kitchen and bathroom jutting out from the otherwise circular room—and put on my maroon leather gloves and earmuffs for a walk.

I hunched my shoulders against the wind as I walked up the hill, around the pond, and back through the dark woods, breathing deeply in a way I never seemed to do when I was fixing dinner for somebody or sending e-mails about the school fundraiser. I'd come to this property many times over two decades, had cross-country skied through the woods, and walked along the hilly gravel roads in all kinds of weather. Once I saw two coyotes run across my path. There was always something life-giving in reconnecting to this land—or any natural place, really. I always felt more peaceful and clearheaded after time away from the city, especially time in the mountains. I knew that time alone in nature was one of the best ways for me to remember who I was, but I didn't always remember to make the time.

Sitting in the geodesic dome at night, I read the journals I'd kept at Pendle Hill as a student nearly twenty years earlier. I was amazed to discover that the issues I was thinking about now were strong themes then. "I *want* to live simply," I'd written, underlining the word "want." I also said I wanted to write about consumerism and the connection between economic and environmental issues, which shocked me since both of my books had been about spiritual discernment. Even when working on the Pendle Hill program on social issues, I wrote in my journal that I yearned for a deeper kind of engagement, one that was more in the streets than behind a computer screen. So the three impulses I was feeling now—to live simply, to write about consumption, and to engage in activism—had been there sharp and clear twenty years ago, though they had been blunted over the years. I headed home from the retreat with a sense that I was grinding down the dull parts of an old blade.

There was a time when my website bio described me as a "writer, mother, teacher, and activist," but three years earlier I had deleted the "activist" from my bio, feeling that I didn't deserve it anymore. In the wake of 9/11 and the invasion of Iraq, I had dragged my children to peace vigils and protest marches—in cold and rainy weather, it often seemed. At one rag-tag event in front of Philadelphia's National Constitution Center, six-year-old Megan looked around at the aging hippies preaching to themselves and said, "This is not going to change George Bush's mind." After a few more such events, I concluded she was right.

Part of what I liked about Earth Quaker Action Team was that they cared about being effective. George in particular seemed allergic to anything as pointless as a rally where we preached to ourselves, so strategy was always part of the conversation. Soon after I joined EQAT, he proposed an ambitious new tactic: a two hundred–mile spring walk across Pennsylvania to build support for our campaign and highlight PNC Bank's role in financing mountaintop removal coal mining. We would call it The Green Walk for Jobs and Justice. Everyone was excited, though it was clearly going to be a lot of work.

At the February monthly meeting, we started by singing a round of "Marching Up the Mountain," written and led by Jonathan Snipes, the redheaded man whose words had moved me after George's speech. Then the energetic organizer, Zack, who was in his twenties, asked everyone to split into the four groups that would plan the details of the Green Walk: action, logistics, press, and networking. That night, each group would gather for just ten minutes to select a facilitator and schedule a time in the next few weeks when the people interested in this aspect of the planning could meet. Zack didn't disclose how big the facilitator role would become over the coming weeks, but I'd done enough volunteering over the years to know a hook when I saw one. I sensed it was my moment to decide whether I was really ready to step up and use some of my gifts in the work against climate change.

As six of us pulled our chairs into a circle on one side of the meeting room, I remembered an incident six years earlier in a different circle. A woman who lived down the block and I had sent out an e-mail inviting our neighbors to discuss defeating our reactionary US senator, Rick Santorum. A surprising number of people had shown up, along with the citywide organizer, who had agreed to fill us in on the campaign and help us get started. As he looked around the packed living room the organizer had asked, "Well, who is your leader?"

The whole room had turned and looked at me, even though I had no official position with the group and most of the people were older than I was. It was the moment I first realized that all my little bits of experience in different forums were gelling into some leadership quality that other people could sense in me, particularly the ability to know what a group needed.

So far, I had never really claimed this gift, though come to think of it, I had been asked to take on leadership roles in virtually every community I had ever been part of, starting in the Girl Scouts. In high school, I was appointed Outing Club President and Yearbook Editor. When I was still new to Quakerism, I was asked to facilitate the meeting where my membership was approved, which I realized in hindsight was quite unorthodox. Since then, I had facilitated many meetings in my congregation and my children's school, where I'd served on the board and led the Religious Life Committee. In recent years, I had declined several requests to serve on various Quaker boards or in other leadership roles. Lately, I had been wondering if these requests were clues about the gifts I was meant to be using.

Back at the EQAT meeting, the six people interested in networking with other environmental and faith groups had circled up. I was happy to see JoAnn, whom I'd worked with on the board of my children's school years earlier. We had also gone to several movies together, including Al Gore's climate change documentary, *An Inconvenient Truth*. JoAnn had a great laugh, a passion for social justice, and zest for life that I appreciated, but I knew she liked to chat at meetings. She had already started sharing her enthusiasm for this work in a way that was both touching and distracting from the tasks we'd be given. We only had a few minutes and clearly needed a facilitator to help us focus.

I took a deep breath and interjected, "I think it would be great to start our first real meeting by sharing our motivation for doing this work, but we only have a few minutes tonight before Zack calls us back." I paused to see that the group was with me. At least a few looked relieved that someone had taken the reins. "Unless there is someone else who wants to do it, I would be willing to be the facilitator," I said. Everyone nodded enthusiastically, especially the board clerk, Carolyn, who already had a large role and was clearly hoping someone else would volunteer for this piece. I urged everyone to get out their calendars before Zack called us back to the big group. We agreed to meet at JoAnn's house in a week.

It was a little step—except that I knew it wasn't.

Chapter Eleven:
Providence Moves Too

Until one is committed, there is hesitancy, the chance to draw back, always ineffectiveness. Concerning all acts of initiative (and creation), there is one elementary truth the ignorance of which kills countless ideas and splendid plans: that the moment one definitely commits oneself, then providence moves too.

—William Hutchinson Murray
(though commonly attributed to Johann Wolfgang von Goethe)

Zack gave me an enthusiastic "awesome!" when he heard I would facilitate the Networking Committee for the Green Walk, the biggest thing Earth Quaker Action Team had attempted in its short history. The other groups had found leaders, too, and he announced that he couldn't be happier with the teams. His next weekly e-mail included a quote popularly attributed to the German thinker and writer Johann Wolfgang von Goethe, asserting that once we made a commitment, providence moved, too. Throughout the planning process, as winter faded into spring, I felt that providence was moving—or as Quakers say, way was opening—on several fronts.

The Sunday after the EQAT meeting where I volunteered to facilitate, the Networking Committee gathered at the home JoAnn and her husband Bill had recently renovated. They'd made it as environmentally friendly as possible, with low-flush toilets, great insulation, and some kind of super energy-efficient fireplace that was halfway up the wall and very chic. As JoAnn gave me a tour, we peered out her large windows at the late-winter landscape, and she lit up as she pointed out where they planned to lay a patio and where her new raised garden beds would be. I had admired JoAnn's extensive vegetable garden at her old house and could only imagine what she would do with this spacious yard. She and Bill were both in their early eighties, and had only been married a few years, but they had the energy and enthusiasm of thirty-year-olds fixing up their first house.

As everyone arrived, we each got a cup of tea and sat down around a beautiful, round wooden table. As was the custom in many Quaker-led organizations, we began the meeting with a few minutes of silence, a practice that always helped me catch my breath. As I closed my eyes and inhaled deeply, I remembered the first time I taught the Discerning· Our Calls class at Pendle Hill, several years earlier. I had been a little nervous beginning something new, but in the opening silence a simple prayer formed in my mind that instantly centered me: "Let me be your instrument. Let this class be your instrument. Let these people be your instruments." The prayer came to me again around JoAnn and Bill's table, so I repeated it silently in my mind, substituting the word "meeting" for "class." I felt a calm assurance that I was where I was meant to be.

After a few minutes, I looked around the small circle and said, "Welcome." I asked each person to share their name and why they were doing this work. I was moved by the depth of everyone's answers, the concern they held for their children and grandchildren, for people in Appalachia, and for the earth. Carolyn, who was a few years older than I was, said she had cut back on her paid work in order to devote more time to addressing climate change. At forty-nine, I was the youngest, but this group showed no signs of being ready to give up on the world.

As we moved into the topic of networking, we brainstormed groups we should invite to join us along the Green Walk, such as faith communities and environmental organizations. We divided up some research, and agreed to meet again in two weeks, this time at my house since JoAnn and Bill were getting ready to go kayaking in the Everglades.

At the next meeting we sat around my dining room table and tried to get clear about what we would be asking people to do. Another committee was working on logistics, arranging hospitality for the walkers, mostly at Quaker meetings. It seemed our job was mostly to recruit large numbers of people for three main events: our launch in Philadelphia, an action in Harrisburg, and a grand finale at PNC's corporate headquarters in Pittsburgh. If people were willing to join the walk for a few days, that was even better, but focusing on those three cities helped as we assigned ourselves more homework.

When JoAnn and Bill got back from the Everglades—with fabulous pictures and stories about the alligators—we all practiced what we would say when we called people to ask them to support our walk. JoAnn and Bill made as many phone calls as anyone—more after I visited one afternoon and taught them how to post the results of their work on a Google Doc the networking committee was using to track our contacts. As my fiftieth birthday approached, I was grateful to spend time with such vivacious octogenarians, who were always ready to try something new. They made aging look like something to embrace rather than fear.

My looming fiftieth birthday had intensified the urgency I felt about living fully myself, along with a few reminders of my mortality. First was Dave's brain tumor, which had come out of the blue. I knew from my weekly walks with Deb that he was doing remarkably well after surgery, but he was a few years younger than I was, a reminder not to wait to fulfill my purpose. Shortly after Dave's diagnosis, an essay went viral on Facebook called, "Five Regrets of the Dying." Written by author and caregiver Bronnie Ware, it asserted that at the end of their lives most people regretted things like not being true to themselves, not following their dreams, and not allowing themselves to be happy.

To hammer the point home, I heard a message in Quaker meeting for worship that felt directed at me. A woman stood one Sunday and spoke about a friend of hers who had a particularly deadly form of cancer. During the glorious year that the cancer was in remission, he had lived fully and deliberately in a way most of us never do. During that year he told the woman, "Whatever you want to do, do it now." That was her message to the meeting: "Do it now."

I came home from worship and journaled about what I would regret not doing if I got a brain tumor next week. Number one on the list was, "Go back to Botswana."

For years I'd wanted to go back. First, I was waiting until we had enough money. By the time we did, my children were unenthused, probably due to my lectures on how my students in Botswana hadn't needed electronics to be happy. I knew my children would love to see live elephants and crocodile in Botswana's game parks, but that wasn't the kind of trip I wanted to take. I wanted to visit old friends in Bobonong and speak Setswana, which would be boring even for Tom, though he was a good enough sport to say he'd go if I wanted him to. With nowhere in the United States to leave our kids, a couple's trip didn't feel viable—at least not as long as our children were still living at home—so I'd suppressed my own yearning to go back.

After the "do it now" message in meeting, it occurred to me that I could just go back to Africa alone. That would cost a lot less money than four plane tickets and probably be more pleasant for everyone. I mentioned it to a few friends, and they were supportive. I brought it up with Tom and he said, "Well, go then."

When I mentioned the trip to Deb on our weekly walk, she wanted to come with me. She and Dave had visited Zambia together, and she had been yearning to return. Our eyes lit up at the prospect of being in Africa together on our birthday, which happened to be the same August day. Of course, I wanted to go to Botswana while Deb wanted to go to Zambia, which was like two African friends planning to visit the United States together when one wanted to visit Rhode Island and the other North Carolina. The logistics were complicated. More importantly, Dave was still getting chemo. I doubted Deb would go if he wasn't 100 percent recovered, but her enthusiasm encouraged me to research plane tickets despite the busyness of planning the Green Walk, which was only a few weeks away by the time Deb admitted that she really couldn't come to Africa. By then, I was committed to going myself.

Once I started planning in earnest, my itinerary fell into place with amazing ease. Tom wanted to take vacation in August to coincide with his mother's birthday party in Wisconsin, so we decided I would go to southern Africa then, when he was already going to be with the kids. I wondered if my in-laws would think I was a bad mother, leaving my kids for two weeks, but I didn't dwell on that possibility. Being away from my husband and children on my fiftieth birthday felt odd but also exciting, an affirmation that I was reclaiming some part of myself, which I had to do alone.

I called Mmadithapelo one day and said, "Guess what?"

"You're coming to Botswana!" she guessed immediately. We both laughed at the thought of seeing each other.

"I'm a big woman now," she warned, laughing about how thin she had been in her twenties. She warned me that Bobonong had changed, too, and that I wouldn't recognize the place. Even she could hardly find the old rondavel where I used to live because everything around it was so much more developed.

"I really want to visit Bobonong, but I wouldn't know where to stay," I said.

"There are B&Bs now, *mma*," she responded. "But Sam Rahube and his wife still live there. They are retired now. I'm sure you could stay with them. I could give them a call if you like."

I gratefully accepted.

Way opened at each step of the planning. I googled Quakers in Botswana, figuring that a small group from a minority religion might enjoy contact with a Quaker from another part of the world and might even know of a cheap place for me to stay in the capital, Gaborone. I sent an e-mail to the woman listed as the meeting contact and got a quick reply. It turned out she and her husband were Americans who had lived in Botswana for years. We had mutual friends, not in Botswana, funnily enough, but in Philadelphia, where she had visited my meeting less than a year earlier. She offered me a place to stay at their home in Gaborone and told me to just let her know when I had figured out the dates.

To get to Botswana, I'd have to fly in and out of South Africa, which had been in the death throes of apartheid in the 1980s. In the years since my brief transit to and from Lesotho, I had studied and taught South African history and made South African friends in grad school, so it seemed silly to pass through again without a real visit. I hadn't been in close contact with anyone there for years, but in another striking coincidence, an old friend who lived in Cape Town got in touch, announcing that she was visiting the United States for the first time in fifteen years and wanted to visit me and Tom. She came and spent the night with us just as I was planning my trip, offering advice and inviting me to her famously beautiful city.

If I was going to travel all that way—a trip with a large carbon cost, after all—I figured I should research climate change while I was in southern Africa and write a few articles about it when I got back. Three more bits of serendipity helped. First, I met Nathan Schneider, editor of *Waging Nonviolence*, who was eager for stories of environmental activism in Africa for his Internet news site. Next, I called my friend Kumi, who was now executive director of Greenpeace International, to ask for the names of South Africans I should interview. Although he was based in Amsterdam, it turned out he would be home in South Africa during my trip, giving us the first chance to see each other in years. Then—just to confirm that way was really opening—author Bill McKibben gave a speech sponsored by Pendle Hill and shared the e-mail address of another South African environmentalist with me afterwards.

Pendle Hill decided to use McKibben's visit as an impetus to gather area environmental leaders for a daylong gathering, and I was asked to be one of the small-group facilitators, along with several others from EQAT. George led us all in an exercise where we were asked to list significant activism milestones over the last several decades on sheets of hanging newsprint. I was encouraged by how full the recent sheets were, and not just because those events were remembered more vividly.

I found it especially encouraging to meet people of faith doing this work. At least three participants at the Pendle Hill gathering were rabbis. Through the Green Walk planning, I had also connected with a group called Interfaith Power and Light (IPL), people of different religions working together to green their congregations while also advocating for legislative change. I wrote a *Huffington Post* article—my third in as many months—that connected our Green Walk to a bike ride PA IPL was planning from the middle of Pennsylvania to Washington, DC. People were literally on the move, and I felt encouraged.

The Green Walk started in Philadelphia on the last Monday of April with breakfast and a few minutes of silent worship at a downtown Quaker meeting. By the time we got to PNC's regional headquarters a few blocks away, there were more than seventy of us, ranging in age from three to eighty-three. The bank locked its doors as we posted the signatures of people pledging to move their money out of PNC if it didn't stop financing mountaintop removal. After Zack gave a brief speech through the megaphone, we began walking in earnest, a van trailing behind with luggage and supplies.

I walked the first five miles and chatted along the way with two mothers and their children, the man I'd seen at the first meeting whose rap sheet was longer than his ponytail, and a recent college grad seeking advice on becoming a writer. It was interesting to see the city on foot, walking through the University of Pennsylvania campus, which I normally only drove past. I realized how often I drove to the Rite Aid or the post office in my own neighborhood, when it really wasn't far to walk. I drove to the gym just to get on a treadmill, come to think of it. Walking on a beautiful spring day with friends seemed like a much better way to get exercise, though of course it took time.

People gradually peeled off, hopping on a train or trolley when it was time for them to head home or back to work. After lunch and a bathroom break at The Gold Standard Café, a popular West Philly restaurant with sympathetic owners, a smaller group headed toward the city limit, which was the goal I'd set for myself. It was less than half of the twelve miles to Swarthmore College, where twenty-eight people would end the first day of the walk. I waved goodbye at the city's edge and took a trolley back to Center City and then a train home where I continued to phone and e-mail potential allies to invite them to join us on the other side of the state.

Although Tom was trying to pick up more on the home front—taking over two of my least favorite jobs, cleaning the bathrooms and tracking permission slips—I didn't feel I could just leave him and the kids to walk across Pennsylvania for seventeen days, especially since I'd be taking a few weeks away during my summer trip to Africa. Instead, I had decided to meet up with the march at a few key points.

I woke early the first Saturday and drove with Tom an hour and a half west to the Lancaster Quaker meetinghouse, where we received warm hugs from George, Walter, Zack, and the others who had been with the walk since Philadelphia. Lancaster Quakers and local environmental activists joined us at the nearest PNC branch where Zack and two people who had worked in Appalachia gave short speeches, while I handed out flyers to passersby, who seemed both curious and supportive. After wrapping the front doors in yellow crime scene tape, we posed in front of them with a circular sign—a caricature of PNC's corporate logo, which normally looked like an orange recycling symbol. Ours had the top shattered into pieces, like the blown-up crown of a mountain.

The circular sign was inspired by 350.org—the global organization cofounded by Bill McKibben and some students from Middlebury College—which took its name from science, 350 parts per million being the amount of carbon dioxide that many scientists believed was safe for the climate. The group had asked people around the world to post photographs of how climate change was affecting their region to help people "connect the dots" between extreme weather and the nearly 400 parts per million of carbon dioxide that were already in the atmosphere. It was hard to illustrate climate change on a beautiful spring day in central Pennsylvania, but I loved the idea of linking the financing of mountaintop removal to what others were experiencing around the world and had convinced EQAT to add a visual dot to our Lancaster action so we could post our photo on 350's site.

After the action and the photo, the walkers continued west, the van still trailing them with supplies, while Tom and I headed home. When I got back to my computer, I scrolled through the pictures that were being posted from around the world: a melting glacier in Bolivia, forest fire destruction in Colorado, flooding in Haiti, and the shrinking of Lake Victoria in Uganda—all linked to climate change.

I had known that burning coal was particularly bad for the climate, which was one of the reasons I had been attracted to EQAT's campaign. It was only after I joined the group that I realized how little I had known about mountaintop removal mining. Since the 1960s, with little attention from people outside of Appalachia, coal companies had destroyed over five hundred mountains and poisoned over two thousand streams just to extract coal seams that would not be profitable to reach through the underground mining that had employed my father's grandfathers in nineteenth-century Pennsylvania. The more I learned about the political control that coal executives exerted in West Virginia, the more it felt like colonialism in Ireland or Africa, where outsiders came and took resources with no concern for the people of the region, who not coincidentally, were savagely stereotyped.

Some Appalachians argued that their mountains could host wind farms, which would provide longer-lasting jobs without poisoning the region's water, but the coal companies wouldn't let that happen. You can make much more money from a limited resource owned by a few than a resource like wind or solar that is free to everyone, so the coal companies didn't want to stop digging until the last black rock was burnt. The same was happening in the gas and oil industries, which were also resorting to extreme extraction techniques, like fracking, which was a more familiar issue for many of the people we encountered as we slowly crossed Pennsylvania. The fossil fuel companies were digging us deeper in terms of climate change, while actively lobbying against renewable alternatives.

My mother's father—the most business savvy of my ancestors—had unwittingly modeled a different way of seeing things. As a blacksmith in the early 1900s, most of his work came from horse owners, but as automobiles grew in popularity, he saw that his business model would not work for his sons, so he had my Uncle Joe study auto mechanics as well. Rather than fighting the inevitable change in our economy, they kept their affluent customers as they transitioned from carriages to automobiles. Unfortunately the fossil fuel industry was not as visionary as my grandfather, who had a fourth-grade education in rural Ireland.

Each night of the Green Walk, Walter and Zack took turns leading an educational session for whatever group was hosting them, often the local Quaker meeting. I was glad that I could dip in and out of the walk without the hours Walter was putting in. A few days after meeting the walkers in Lancaster, Joann and I drove out to Harrisburg to join the group in pouring spring rain. The group had held actions at PNC branches every day, finding supporters in small towns and along the roads. In the state capital, we were also joined by local Catholics and Unitarians, a representative of the Pennsylvania Council of Churches, and the Pennsylvania head of the Sierra Club, who announced from under an umbrella that they would close their account with PNC if the bank didn't change its policies.

I was happy with the turnout, especially given the weather, though a few of the local people were nervous about the advertised "die in" to dramatize those dying from cancer in Appalachia. I wasn't sure if Zack was going to pull that off in the driving rain, but he was so convincing when speaking about the tragedy of mountaintop removal that almost every person lay down on the wet sidewalk, including JoAnn and the other people in their seventies and eighties. I lay between them, feeling the rain through my blue cashmere sweater, and wondering how long Zack planned to keep us there as he continued to speak passionately from the bank steps about the death toll from cancer. As I felt a sidewalk puddle saturate my sleeve, I caught Zack's eye and made a circular wrap-it-up motion with my index finger.

· Without missing a beat, Zack said, "And we will rise from the ashes like the people of Appalachia." His voice rose as he motioned for us to stand up, which everyone did in surprisingly good spirits.

At the end of the seventeen-day walk, I drove across the Pennsylvania mountains to join EQAT in Pittsburgh for our grand climax. On the last morning, we filled the wraparound porch of the Quaker meetinghouse with people ready to walk the last three miles. In addition to the two EQAT members who had walked all two hundred miles, there were Quakers from across the state, allies from West Virginia, people of different faiths, and a variety of environmental groups. One local woman brought an enormous banner that said, "You Can't Drink Money!" There was a cyclist who was planning "Tour de Frack," a ride from Butler County, Pennsylvania to Washington, DC to lobby legislators about fracking. It was a perfect spring day, and by the time we reached PNC's corporate headquarters, there were seventy-five of us, as well as a line of police. I was assigned to speak to the small group of reporters with pads, microphones, and cameras.

Although George had said at the beginning that he was game for committing civil disobedience at PNC's corporate headquarters, the group had decided not to have anyone risk arrest on a day when so many of us were tired from the walk and far from home. Still, we wanted to make it clear that we were not just another bunch of stand-in-the-wind protestors who would show up once and leave it at that. After waves of people attempted to deliver a meeting invitation to PNC's CEO, James Rohr, Zack conducted a training in civil disobedience right on the sidewalk in front of PNC's corporate headquarters. Half the group sat down and role-played getting arrested, while the other half played the police with the real police watching bemused from the sidelines. We sang "This Little Light of Mine"—an old hymn used in the civil rights movement, like many of the songs EQAT sang.

When the action was over, and we were preparing to head back to Philadelphia, the Tour de Frack organizer said to me enthusiastically, "People in our group probably aren't going to do stuff like that, but seeing you all do it will make them bolder when it's time to speak up in a meeting."

EQAT was bold but also respectful. We were polite to the police, while not backing down. Tactics were creative and fun, but also filled with a serious message, like the windmills the group built in a PNC lobby the week before I joined. George never missed an opportunity to point out that it was such nonviolent direct action that had historically won the most gains, not letter writing and petitions. I was convinced.

While the antiwar protests I had attended after the invasion of Iraq never felt like they had a chance of changing Bush's policies, our creative actions had gotten PNC's attention. They had sent their general counsel to meet with student activists at UPenn and Temple. Their website no longer described them as a green bank with Quaker roots, a sign we were having an impact on their marketing. Because we were doing something different, we were getting in the news, which we knew mattered to a bank that invested a lot in its corporate image.

Helping to organize the Green Walk employed many of the same skills I'd used fundraising for the Costa Rica Exchange Program: the ability to see what needs to be done and recruit volunteers to do it, the facility to run a meeting, a willingness to send a lot of e-mails and make a few phone calls, a desire to do a good job, and a sense of personal responsibility. What was different was the joy I felt working with this group. The powerful singing continued to feel symbolic of the positive energy I felt when we came together, and though I wasn't one of the best singers, I felt my own vocal cords gradually opening up. I remembered the Buechner quote I used in my discernment course: "The place God calls you to is the place where your deep gladness and the world's deep hunger meet."

When Carolyn called to ask me to join the EQAT board, I said yes immediately. When someone from my children's school asked if I would organize the food for graduation, I answered a resounding no.

As planning for the spring trip across Pennsylvania ended, planning for my summer trip to Africa picked up. Figuring out how to get to Mmadithapelo turned out to be the trickiest part. Orapa—a diamond mining town in a remote part of Botswana—was a nine-hour drive from Johannesburg, and a much longer bus ride. There weren't any direct flights, unless you worked for the mining company. Mmadithapelo said she could sometimes hitch a ride by plane, which made me laugh because I could just see her, friendly but assertive, talking her way onto the company jet. But it wasn't something you could count on, she said.

I tried searching for flights from Johannesburg to Francistown, the Botswana city closest to Orapa, but found nothing. Then, at the EQAT party celebrating the Green Walk, I ran into a Quaker who used to live in Botswana. She told me there were flights, but only on Tuesdays and Thursdays, a detail I would never have figured out from CheapTickets. I went home and booked a Tuesday flight to Francistown, as well as a rental car, which I could return in South Africa for an extra fee. I was still trying to figure out how to do interviews about climate change, and the car would make it easier to visit rural areas in both countries, I realized.

When I told Mmadithapelo my plan and the time my afternoon flight would arrive in Francistown, she warned me not to make the three-hour drive to Orapa after dark.

"There are animals on that road," she said ominously, which I enjoyed repeating to friends for dramatic effect, though I later found out she meant mostly cattle, which were as deadly as lion if you hit one at high speed. Lots of people told me I was brave, and it occurred to me that a certain daring probably was one of my gifts. Maybe that was part of why I felt called to work with EQAT rather than Transition Town, I thought, so I could use that part of myself that was willing to do things that other people found scary.

To me, the trip was far more exciting than daunting. Still, I was nervous about the three-hour drive through what I imagined as a snake-filled desert where there would be no Starbucks if I needed to pee—the sort of thing a forty-nine-year-old woman thought about a lot more than her younger self. I could understand how people got stuck in comfortable ruts, never doing anything risky. At every step it would have been easier to just let the idea drop and head to Wisconsin with Tom and the kids. As my involvement with EQAT increased, I wondered if this trip was a way of exercising my courage muscles for whatever else was coming next in my life.

A member of my Quaker meeting suggested that I should have a support committee, a tool Quakers sometimes used, especially when doing something scary or when in need of spiritual grounding. I picked a Saturday night in July, which Tom predicted would be a terrible time, so I invited twice as many people as were necessary. To our surprise, most came, and a loving circle of thirteen friends joined Tom and me in our oppressively hot living room. Most but not all were Quakers. Almost half had traveled in Africa, including Dave and Deb.

I told them about the strong pull I felt to go back to southern Africa and the things I had already learned, such as the fact that South Africa was expecting water shortages in the coming decades, but in a crisis, the new coal plants they were building would get water before the surrounding villagers. The group listened and speculated about whether it would be dangerous for me to take photographs of the power plants, a possibility that made Tom look slightly ill. Vanessa Julye offered to lend me a silk sleeping bag liner since it was winter in the Southern Hemisphere, where most people didn't heat their houses as much as we did. Vanessa's husband, Barry Scott, offered to set up a schedule through a Doodle poll, so there would be at least one person holding me in prayer each day of my trip.

Near the end, Walter's wife, Traci, suggested they pray over me, which was uncommon but not unheard of for contemporary Quakers. I moved my chair to the center of the living room and closed my eyes. I felt hands touch my back and shoulders as one friend after another offered their blessings, prayed for my safety, my faithfulness, and my marriage. Tears filled my eyes as Traci ended with a song of blessing.

"That's where God is," Deb had said seven months earlier when I'd tearily reported my yearning to use my gifts. She'd been right, but God was also here, in my feeling of connection to other people, as well as the serendipity that kept emerging. Although I found myself talking about God and spirituality less than I had when I was writing about those topics, I felt more connected to a higher purpose than I had in some time.

In our last phone call before I left, I asked Mmadithapelo what I could bring her children as gifts, and she mentioned that her son

Mopati had recently lost his guitar when it fell off the back of a truck and broke at the neck. Mopati was a serious musician, but the thought of buying him a guitar and carrying it all the way to Orapa felt pretty inconvenient, so I changed the subject. Then that night Tom mentioned that one of his friends from church, who was an excellent but aging musician, was giving away a very good guitar and wanted it to go to someone who would really appreciate it.

"Do we know anyone who would want a guitar?" Tom asked.

It seemed like more of the way opening that was appearing at every turn, so I said, "Yes."

Early one morning in late July, Tom drove me to JFK airport, along with my wheeled carry-on bag, a grey knapsack, and the guitar for Mopati. Tom nervously kissed me goodbye, and I promised to e-mail when I could from the iPad he had lent me. As I entered the terminal, I could feel my heart beating fast.

Chapter Twelve:
Utterly Untenable

We've globalized an utterly untenable economic model of
hyperconsumerism. It's now successfully spreading
across the world, and it's killing us.
—Naomi Klein

A s I flew into Francistown, I looked out the plane window at the winding, dry bed of the Shashi River, which flowed—for only a few days per year—southeast into the Limpopo River, where Botswana, Zimbabwe, and South Africa met. By the time I got through Botswana customs, the sun was low on the dusty horizon, and I was glad I had planned to stay in Francistown for the night before making the isolated three-hour drive to Mmadithapelo in Orapa.

A Motswana man led me out to my rental car, a white Toyota Camry just like the one I drove in Philadelphia, except that—because I'd be driving on the left side of the road—everything was reversed, with the wheel on the right side. I loaded my luggage and the guitar in the trunk and set out from the airport past a billboard for cell phones, careful to stay on the left side of a bridge that crossed the dry Shashi River, where a small herd of cattle roamed aimlessly on the sand. I concentrated furiously when I hit my first traffic circle, following the cars clockwise instead of counterclockwise. I wasn't used to the reversed consol either, so every time I went to signal a turn, I activated my windshield wipers—this in a country that hadn't seen rain in months.

Francistown had obviously grown in the twenty-six years since I'd been gone. There were big hotels and casinos, though I'd opted for a small "bush lodge" just outside of town, which advertised wireless Internet on its website. Following the directions I'd printed at home, I passed a strip mall that looked vaguely familiar, though the buildings were bigger than I remembered. There were many, many more cars, but people still walked along the edge of the road. Trying not to hit anyone, I missed my turn and ended up in an eerily quiet industrial park just as it was getting dark. When I finally got myself oriented and pulled into the dirt lot of the Dumela Lodge, I sighed in relief.

The lodge itself was a one-story building elevated four feet off the ground on wooden stilts with a high thatched roof. Inside were an empty restaurant, a bar, and two young African men watching the Olympics on the flat-screen television that hung on the wall below the grass ceiling. The desk clerk welcomed me warmly, laughing when I greeted him in Setswana. He told me to pull my car around, past the cold-looking swimming pool, to a platform tent twenty-five yards away, part of a circle of tents that had been advertised as "chalets" on the website.

The platform tent reminded me of the ones at Girl Scout camp, with green canvas sides that could be rolled up in nicer weather, except that it also had a wooden door with a small key, a toilet, a sink, a bath-tub, an electric space heater, and a television that played five different Christian channels. Looking at the ring of tents around me, I seemed to be the only customer on this cold, off-season night. After watching the light fade over the surrounding bush, I followed the path back to the lodge and sat at the bar.

The first young man, who said his name was Zazi, brought me a Lion, the South African beer that had lubricated my Peace Corps experience, though now it was much better chilled than it had ever been in Bobonong's village bar. Since beef was Botswana's specialty, I ordered a hamburger and savored it while chatting in English with Zazi and David, the cook, who stood nearby, glancing occasionally at the Olympics. For the first time in my life, it struck me that the summer Olympics took place while the more populated southern half of the globe was experiencing winter. I felt silly that I hadn't noticed before.

I mentioned that on my way there I had crossed the Shashi River, and it was completely dry. "That is normal this time of year, right?" I asked.

"Oh, yes," said Zazi. "It's the dry season, so that's normal. It never rains this time of year," though after a pause he added that it had actually rained during the dry season last year, and for the past few years it hadn't rained when it was supposed to. "The weather is getting weird," he observed.

Zazi and David told me how the farmers had been confused the previous spring when the rains didn't come until well over a month late. Many of them didn't even bother planting. It was terrible.

"But it's not just here," said David, who was originally from Zimbabwe.

"Yeah, it's that global warming thing," interjected Zazi, nodding. I agreed, adding that it was summer in the United States now and American farmers were experiencing a terrible drought. Many were losing their crops.

"There are farmers in America?" asked David surprised. I laughed, knowing that he got his picture of the United States from television shows like *Law & Order* while Americans were getting their picture of Africa from *The Lion King*.

Yes, I told him, lots of food was grown in the United States, and many farmers had been hurt by the drought. His brow crinkled, his compassion palpable. I knew Zimbabwe's harsh colonial legacy had been followed by corrupt leadership and a bungled attempt at land reform, leading to devastating food shortages only a few years earlier. That was probably why David was working in Botswana.

"How are things in Zimbabwe these days?" I asked gingerly.

"Oh, much better now," he said. "Much better now." Zazi nodded in agreement.

David and Zazi became more reserved when I was joined at the bar by a middle-aged white man, a diamond drill salesman en route to Zambia, whose accent sounded South African. He ordered a steak, and David retreated to the kitchen. Eager to check e-mail, I pulled out Tom's iPad, which had a keyboard that doubled as a case.

"I have an iPad, too," said the man eagerly. "Where did you get that keyboard? The only thing I don't like about the iPad is that it's hard to type on."

"It's really my husband's," I said self-consciously. "We ordered the case off of Amazon for Father's Day. You're right. It does make it easier to type."

He looked disappointed. "I've heard of Amazon. It hasn't come to Africa yet. I'd really like a keyboard like that."

I could already see after only a few hours that Botswana was not quite caught up to the United States technologically, but it was much closer than it had been in the eighties. Still the laid-back Botswana I had loved was not totally gone. After several failed attempts to get online, I asked Zazi for help, and he shrugged, unconcerned.

"Sometimes the wireless works. Sometimes it doesn't work."

Slightly disappointed, I walked past the deserted pool to my cold tent, imagining how fun it would be to sleep with the sides rolled up in warmer weather—maybe with Tom and the kids someday. In the morning, the woman who had replaced Zazi at the desk let me use the Internet on her desktop computer before I checked out, so I e-mailed Tom and my support committee to tell them I had arrived in Botswana safely and was on my way to Orapa.

The three-hour drive was much less menacing than I'd anticipated, though I was right that there was no Starbucks. I passed brown bush, an occasional cluster of rondavels sprinkled along the road, and a surprising number of hitchhikers. Most were going from one cluster of houses to the next, so I stopped to offer rides to as many as I could, starting with two elementary school–aged sisters who spoke no English—payback, I figured, for all the rides I'd hitched during my Peace Corps days. My last passengers of the morning were a young woman and her feverish baby. Her husband worked in the mine, the mother explained, so they were on their way to the Orapa clinic for treatment.

When we arrived at the imposing Orapa gates, I parked in front of the security office while a woman located my permit, took my photograph, and called Mmadithapelo to let her know I'd arrived. The woman with the baby showed their papers, and we were waved through to what felt like an elaborate gated community, with neat subdivisions and curbs painted like candy canes in the quaint "downtown." Mmadithapelo thought it would be easier for me to find the supermarket than her house, so we met out front, squealing when we spotted each other. We gave each other a long, rocking hug, then laughed out loud at the sight of each other. We both had longer hair and wider middles, but were instantly recognizable.

We hopped in my Toyota and, after dropping the woman and the baby at the clinic, drove a few minutes to Mmadithapelo's comfortable three-bedroom home. I parked under the portico, and she showed me around her sizeable yard, where she intended to plant some fruit trees. She had been issued this house, not because she was a big wig in the company, which she wasn't, but because she had two children. Housing, she explained, was assigned according to need and subsidized by the mine, along with electric and water. In a month, she paid less for rent, electric, and water combined than we paid for water alone. She praised the Orapa primary school her children had attended, as well as the medical care she received as a mine employee. Since her divorce, this job had been a lifesaver.

I smiled, thinking of a friend in Philadelphia who'd heard I would be staying in an African diamond mining town and immediately pictured the gruesome scenes depicted in the film *Blood Diamond*, about the deadly diamond wars in West Africa. Mmadithapelo's comfortable living room couldn't have been further from those horrific images. Sitting on her plush couch, we fell into easy conversation, looking at pictures of our children and eating the favorite Tswana foods she had prepared for me—*seswaa, morogo wa dinawa*, and *phaleche* (mashed beef, greens with peanut butter, and the thick corn meal that was the country's staple).

She asked me what else I had planned for my week in Botswana, and I confessed that my plans were loose. I wanted to look up old friends, but I also wanted to interview people about climate change, and I wasn't sure how I was going to do both, given that the capital was a six-hour drive from Orapa. Mmadithapelo had arranged to take four days off work for my visit. As I'd hoped, she agreed to join me on a road trip, which would also give her the chance to introduce me to her daughter Tshego, a college sophomore, and her son Mopati, a high school student at a boarding school near Gaborone. We agreed to leave in the morning.

For the next three days, we enjoyed a whirlwind of driving and visits. The Quaker couple in Gaborone hosted us and brought us to the opening of an exhibit of art by Zimbabwean refugees. Mmadithapelo's daughter Tshego showed us around the University of Botswana, which now had 18,000 students. At the end of our university tour, we stopped by the counseling office of Chris Tidimane, son of the family who had hosted me at their lands when I was trying to improve my Setswana. I'd found him on LinkedIn.

Chris had decided we should surprise his father, who now lived with him in town since his mother's passing. The old man looked confused when Mmadithapelo and I walked into the living room, and I was seated next to him on the couch. After a minute Mr. Tidimane's eyes widened in recognition, and he said, "Nchadi?"—the Setswana name his family had given me decades ago. I grinned and nodded. He glanced at my streaks of grey hair and said in English, "You're old now," which made everyone laugh. Chris was very pleased with himself for pulling off the surprise and gathered in his children and sister, one of my former students, for a group photo on the couch.

The next morning in Gaborone, I left Mmadithapelo sleeping in the room we were sharing and drove around looking for the Meteorology Department, the government office charged with monitoring the weather and climate. Like most places in Botswana, it had a lot number and a post office box but not an actual street address. I'd been warned not to use my iPhone map because of expensive roving charges, so I left early enough to get lost and get a cup of coffee at a nearby hotel, both of which I did before pulling into the fenced parking lot with my notebook full of questions. I asked the receptionist for Botswana's principal meteorologist, Dorcas Masisi, and was led to her office. A middle-aged Motswana, she sat across the desk. A young German man working with her as part of a governmental exchange sat in the chair beside me.

"It's not just that the average temperature has risen," she explained in English. "There are fewer days with the minimum temperature. The maximum temperature is rising. The extreme high used to be 42°C"—which I later calculated was 107.6°F—"Now that's not an extreme," she said matter-of-factly. She confirmed what I had heard at the Dumela Lodge, that the rains had been late and sporadic, sometimes a whole season's worth deluging in one day with no more the rest of the season.

"If you plant, it will wither," she said.

I asked what Botswana was doing in response to this growing threat, and the young German scientist jumped in, clearly more comfortable than Dorcas Masisi criticizing the government's response.

"There is some talk about climate change," he acknowledged, "but it is insufficient. There needs to be a clear vision." He argued that because Botswana mined and burned coal, it was tempting to keep developing that resource, even though it added carbon dioxide to the atmosphere. He believed investing in coal was also shortsighted because it would be less economical in the future, if the world ever adopted a tax on carbon emissions, which many environmentalists advocated. With Botswana's abundant sun and relatively empty land, it was ideal for more projects like the solar farm that was currently under construction in the south of the country with aid from the Japanese government.

Dorcas Masisi interjected that foreign aid was necessary for such large-scale projects, but that there were many small-scale adaptation programs going on across the country, such as building windbreaks to avoid water losses and encouraging people to go back to the indigenous crop, sorghum, rather than maize, which she described as "the terrible one" in terms of drought.

My interview with Dorcas Masisi confirmed what I was hearing outside the Meteorology Department. As I picked up hitchhikers on each leg of my journey, the same conversation played over and over: "The rains were late last year. Many farmers didn't even bother planting. The weather is getting weird." What had changed in the past few decades was not that people were anxious about the lack of rain—that was perennial in Botswana. It was that the weather had become unpredictable, erratic, "weird." People knew how to cope with drought, but this? Everyone agreed the situation was bad. The only variable was whether the speaker understood that their weather was part of a global problem that was predicted to get worse.

One hitchhiker—an old man who spoke in Setswana through Mmadithapelo—said that the bad weather came from burning coal, though it wasn't clear to me if he understood that my country's long history of burning coal had contributed to the problem much more than his. I thought of climate change deniers at home who claimed that global warming was a liberal fiction invented to justify big government and wondered how they'd explain this old African farmer, who was clearly reading the land, not *The New York Times*.

On our last afternoon in Gaborone, Mmadithapelo and I set off for her son Mopati's school. I'd lugged Mopati's guitar from JFK to Gaborone in what turned out to be an extremely heavy guitar case. When we finally arrived at his boarding school, annoyance disappeared as I saw him pull out the guitar and start strumming with a shy smile. We staged some pictures of Mopati and the guitar, a photograph being the only payment its previous owner wanted. Mmadithapelo jumped into a few of the shots, proudly putting her arm around her teenage son, who was slightly taller than she was, even with her sizeable Afro. A few of Mopati's high school friends gathered around, and a girl with an angelic face started singing a Setswana church hymn with a pure joy that brought tears to my eyes, though I didn't remember enough Setswana to understand the words.

I never did have time to study the moldy Setswana books I'd kept in the basement all those years. Instead I'd downloaded a Setswana app onto my iPhone before I came, but it wasn't much use other than for making Mmadithapelo laugh and say, "Oh my God!" The basic greetings I had remembered, anyway. Each day in Botswana brought back another word or two, so by the time we headed back north toward Orapa, I remembered enough Setswana to talk my way out of a speeding ticket when I got pulled over by the police at a speed trap.

"Go and humble yourself now," Mmadithapelo said when we saw the policeman motioning for me to get out of the car. The hitchhikers in the backseat nodded.

I bowed my head and shoulders as I said, "*Dumela, rra,*" contritely, then strung together every Setswana phrase I could remember, ending with "*Ke rata Botswana.*" ("Hello, sir. . . . I love Botswana.") The policeman waved me on amused.

En route to Orapa, Mmadithapelo and I stopped in the sprawling village of Serowe to see our old neighbor, Mosetsana, who ran out to the road to meet us with the same gap-toothed smile I remembered. I always thought Mosetsana was particularly beautiful, with smooth dark skin, large eyes, and a charming gap between her front teeth. She still looked the same, only with long dreadlocks hanging down from her headscarf and the slightest trace of crow's-feet beneath glasses, which were also new. It was hard to believe she was a grandmother, but baby Kefilwe, who'd lived with us in Bobonong, now had a toddler of her own watching us with big eyes as he gripped a toy car made from wire and soda cans.

Mosetsana was helping to cook at her parents' compound where an old Tswana tradition was taking place. Two young people had gotten engaged, and their families were formally meeting for the first time. It was a big production with lots of traditional rules and food, reminding me of the ceremony I'd attended with the Tidimanes so many moons ago. Mmadithapelo and I were led around and formally introduced to several old women sitting on blankets beneath a tree before being brought over to greet the men, sitting on chairs a short distance away. After everyone had said, "*Dumela*" to us, we were ushered behind the house to the outdoor kitchen for some sorghum and meat.

The middle-aged women were keeping the food warm over a small fire, the kind Mosetsana used to cook over every night in Bobonong, though now she stood chatting on her cell phone, flashing me her gap-toothed smile whenever she remembered I was there. After the elders released her, she brought us to see her house on a hill, a comfortable brick home that could easily belong in an American subdivision, equipped with electricity and running water, as most homes now seemed to be. A retired immigration worker, she had done well and wanted me to see it. Surveying the surrounding homes, I noticed how much bigger they were than in the eighties, many compounds including both a sizable modern house and an old, mud hut, like the one I had loved.

As we prepared to leave Serowe, Mosetsana gave us a tour of her impressive vegetable garden, rows and rows of collards, bright green during a mild winter. I saw a large rain barrel and hose, and Mmadithapelo explained that the current president had started a program to encourage backyard gardens. The government provided materials for fencing, seeds, rain barrel, and a hose. They'd even help you dig if you asked. Mosetsana nodded in agreement. It was part of an initiative to increase food security, and I was impressed.

I hadn't noticed the vegetable gardens when I'd first arrived in

Orapa, but when I returned with Mmadithapelo, I spotted green veggies sprouting behind some of the neat homes near hers. After warm baths, we washed my clothes in her washing machine and then hung them on her clothesline, where they dried quickly in the arid air. When I woke at 5:30 a.m. to say goodbye before she left for work, I found Mmadithapelo had ironed all my clothes before the sun came up.

"Oh, *mma!*" I scolded. "Why did you wake so early? I don't even iron my clothes at home." She shrugged. It was a parting gift.

I walked her to the bus stop, where miners in hardhats were already waiting for the coach that would take them to the actual mine a few miles away. I took a final photo of Mmadithapelo smiling in her green suit uniform and promised to mail her a pair of sneakers from the States since she was trying to exercise more, and good sneakers were prohibitively expensive in Botswana. She promised to have a dress made for me out of the blue-and-white Herero fabric I had always loved, but which I hadn't seen this trip. We hugged goodbye, knowing that cell phones and e-mail would help us stay in better touch this time.

"*Ba dumadisa!*" she said, a common Setswana salutation that means roughly, "Say hello to your people for me." I nodded and waved goodbye as the bus pulled up, feeling confident that it would not be another twenty-five years before we saw each other again.

I walked back to Mmadithapelo's house and the white Toyota, no longer nervous about the road to Francistown, where I would stop for lunch and wireless access before continuing three more hours southeast to the village that had felt like home so long ago.

This time I entered Bobonong in a rental car on a tarred road far less bumpy than the dirt track I'd arrived on in 1984. "My" rondavel was now a storage room for the bed and breakfast that had replaced Mmadithapelo's two-room cinder block house. The people who ran it gave me a tour and smiled as, out of curiosity, I measured the diameter of the rondavel as seventeen and a half steps in my black leather shoes, not counting the modern bathroom that had been added on one side. With a taller fence and no pit latrine, the whole compound looked so different I'd driven up and down the road several times before recognizing the place. I would have given up if Mmadithapelo hadn't assured me it was still there.

My school was equally transformed with a spiffier paint job, lockers, and several new buildings, including a computer lab. My host, Mr. Rahube—the South African deputy head who had eventually become headmaster of the school—looked the same, just with deeper creases in his large forehead. He gave me a tour of the school and introduced me to the current head, the woman who had taken over when he'd retired. She showed us with pride the large plastic cisterns she had gotten for the teacher housing, despite popular misgivings when she first proposed the idea. She explained that because the school was on a hill, the plumbing stopped working when the water table got low, which had been happening more lately, so now people were grateful for her foresight in storing extra water. Mr. Rahube and I posed for a photo in front of a sign in the middle of the schoolyard that said, "Save Water. Save Life. Every Drop Counts."

Like most Batswana, Mr. Rahube kept some land and cattle himself. My first night staying with him and his wife in Bobonong, they confirmed what I'd heard from hitchhikers, that things at the cattle post were "very bad." They'd tried to dig a borehole to get water, but after a hundred meters they still hadn't hit any. One cow could drink fifty liters on a hot day, they said, and of course it needed to eat, too. They'd had to buy feed for the cattle because the grass was so poor, an extra expense that not everyone could afford. Mr. Rahube was curious about my climate change research and offered to help.

"Maybe I'll learn something, too," he said with a chuckle.

The next morning he drove me to the Ministry of Agriculture office for the region surrounding Bobonong. We had no appointment, but to everyone's surprise, it turned out the tall, young man in charge of helping people with their crops had been one of Mr. Rahube's students years ago. Anthony Keeme welcomed us warmly and offered us chairs in his modest office. After a few opening pleasantries, he corroborated what I'd been hearing across Botswana.

"We used to get some rains in September," he explained. "Last year they came late October and November."

Not only that, but sometimes a whole season's worth of rain came at once, he confirmed, which was just as bad for the crops as no rain at all. Also, the winters weren't cold enough to kill the pests, contributing to a dismal food output the previous year. The government was encouraging people to grow sorghum instead of maize, since it was more drought resistant, though it was also more work for the farmers and people didn't like it as much as corn. While some areas had done better than others during the last growing season, on average farmers had gotten only one bag of sorghum per hectare, about 2.5 acres.

"Maize was a disaster," said Anthony Keeme, echoing Dorcas Masisi, who had called maize "the terrible one."

I wondered how people were surviving, given that their two main food sources, crops and cattle, were both in trouble. I asked delicately if anyone was starving to death in Botswana. Both men laughed.

"No, no one starves in Botswana," said Mr. Rahube, who had chosen to stay in Bobonong even after apartheid ended, when he could have gone home to South Africa. "If people's crops fail, their families help them. If the families can't help, the government gives them food aid. No one starves," he assured me. His former pupil nodded.

At the end of our interview, Anthony Keeme led us out to the long garage to show us the enormous tractors and tilling machines, available for any local resident who requested help plowing their fields. He and Mr. Rahube posed proudly in front of a towering red tractor, and I took a picture on my iPhone.

I had heard that poor governance caused famine as much as poor crops, but it wasn't until this trip that I truly appreciated what a life-saving difference a responsive government made. When Botswana became independent in 1966, they had only twenty-two college graduates and twelve kilometers of tarred road in the whole country, but they had leaders who didn't forget the traditional Tswana concern for the common good. The new government had partnered with the South African diamond conglomerate De Beers, which had the technical expertise and capital to extract Orapa's newly discovered diamonds. Botswana's share of the profits went into roads, hospitals, and schools, bringing in international volunteers like myself to staff them until there were enough educated Batswana to take over. Given how few white people I'd seen this trip, it seemed the strategy had been successful.

I'd been surprised by how much I'd liked Orapa, with its quaint red-and-white candy-striped curbs and little Internet café. I'd been skeptical of the mine's claims of a superior safety record, but Mmadithapelo confirmed that Debstwana (the partnership between the government and De Beers) took miner safety very seriously. An Orapa miner we picked up on our way back from Gaborone said the same. On my way to Bobonong, I gave a ride to another miner, a burly man who praised the safety of the copper mine where he worked in Selibe-Pikwe. When I confessed that I thought of mines as dark, dangerous places, he laughed.

"It's nice down there," he insisted. "It's like a city with lots of lights."

I speculated that the Botswana government's early decision to share the nation's wealth had humanized the way they produced that wealth. Still, Orapa was not completely without controversy. Its development had displaced a community of San people, traditional hunter-gatherers, often known by the derogatory term "Bushmen." The San had lived in southern Africa for tens of thousand of years and were believed to be the closest genetic descendants of the world's first humans. The larger and pastoral Batswana had migrated to the region only several hundred years ago, pushing the San into the desert. Some scholars argued that the demographic dominance of the Batswana had made it easier for the government to share the country's mineral wealth, since people often feel more comfortable sharing with their own, though I continued to believe that having a less shattering colonial experience than their neighbors had also helped.

In addition to the dispossession of the San, there was one other problem with mining in Botswana. Extractive industries—those businesses that dig stuff out of the ground and sell it—use a lot of water. In addition to diamonds, Botswana mined copper, nickel, soda ash, and coal. Botswana hadn't burnt much coal compared to my own country, which had been at it since before my father's ancestors fled the Great Hunger and found new livelihoods mining in the anthracite region of Pennsylvania. Botswana didn't burn much compared to its southern neighbor either, South Africa being the largest carbon-emitter in Africa with its large population and industrialized economy. Still, when I drove past the tall, thin towers of a Botswana coal plant, I felt a little sad. This smart, friendly country, which did so many things well, was following a model of development that was making its weather weird and its water even more scarce.

It had been good to see that Mmadithapelo and Mosetsana now had electricity and running water in their houses, though I couldn't help but notice that Mmadithapelo left the tap running like an American while she was doing dishes, and the Rahubes left the Olympics playing on television pretty much nonstop. Maybe becoming like Americans was the whole point of this development business, and I could see why. All these conveniences were nice, and I felt a bit foolish for my wistful memories of carrying water on my head and reading by kerosene lamp, the youthful adventure of a white woman who chose simplicity as an exotic adventure.

Still, I couldn't help noting the connection between Botswana's mode of development and its difficulties. Twenty-five years ago, I'd had to schlep my water from a village tap, but there had always been enough. Now people had indoor plumbing, flush toilets, and washing machines, but Mr. Rahube said that Bobonong ran out of water for days at a time. Compostable toilets—which can be built indoors and don't smell when made correctly—would have made much more sense, though that wouldn't have fit the picture of "development" and ever-increasing consumption promoted by the West.

When I'd mentioned these thoughts to Mmadithapelo she said, "Well, you Americans have had all these things long enough to see the downside of them. We Batswana are just starting to enjoy them, so we still want to have what you have."

I couldn't say I blamed her. It was only after I left Bobonong and headed on a back road to the South African border that I realized that I had been too busy watching the Olympics each night to step outside and look for the Southern Cross.

Chapter Thirteen:
Nothing Exists Alone

In nature nothing exists alone.
—Rachel Carson

The famous Limpopo River looked smaller than its reputation, but at least it was flowing as I drove across the bridge that led from Botswana to South Africa. Farms were bigger and greener on this side of the border, many with large cisterns and wide metal contraptions that I assumed were irrigation machines in a region known for its tea, maize, and mangos. Although apartheid had ended eighteen years earlier, land reform had been protracted, and most such farms were still owned by whites.

Down the road from the green fields I saw one of the "informal settlements" that still existed, shacks of corrugated tin and rubbish packed so tightly they appeared to be holding each other up. They looked like those the Irish priest had shown me when I passed through South Africa twenty-eight years earlier, except that now I saw electric wire running overhead, though I'd heard that many residents couldn't afford the service and tapped the wires illegally. I slowed my rental car down and tried to take a picture discretely.

As I headed south, I saw occasional hitchhikers, but Mmadithapelo had made me promise that I wouldn't pick up anyone in South Africa.

"You'll see a woman by the side of the road, and you'll stop to be nice," she had said in a serious tone. "Then her man will jump out of the bushes and rob you, or worse." So many Africans had warned me about crime in South Africa that I kept my eyes on the road as I passed a weary-looking middle-aged woman with bundles at her feet.

I had decided to drive from Bobonong to Johannesburg in order to see Limpopo Province, which I had come to think of as the Appalachia of South Africa. Known for its stunning mountains and its valuable minerals—particularly coal, iron ore, and platinum—Limpopo was one of the poorest provinces in the country. As in Appalachia, mining had been established to make as much money as possible for a few people with no regard for the land or the laborers. The difference between its history and neighboring Botswana's felt palpable.

Of course, not all South African history was depressing. I had watched the television coverage along with the rest of the world in 1990 as a stately, waving Nelson Mandela walked out of prison after twenty-seven years. I still got teary whenever I saw that footage. It was one of those iconic moments when the impossible was suddenly happening, like the Berlin Wall coming down a few months earlier. When Mandela was elected president in 1994 in the first multiracial elections, many South Africans had danced in the streets.

Given the brutal conditions he'd faced in prison, it was all the more amazing that Mandela had advocated reconciliation. He famously invited the widows of former apartheid prime ministers to tea with widows from his own party, the African National Congress, and embraced rugby—a sport traditionally more popular with Afrikaners, the ethnic group dominant during apartheid. Despite the symbolic power of such gestures, Mandela faced a thorny problem. If he nationalized the mines or redistributed the land, as some members of his party wanted, reconciliation with whites would be impossible, not to mention friendly relations with countries like the United States. Instead of an economic revolution that risked more years of bloodshed or the kinds of problems Zimbabwe had faced, he and the ANC chose reform, seeking international investment and aid for incremental projects, like building more housing for the country's poorest.

Since Mandela's election, the black middle class had prospered as well as a small black elite, but as I could see from the tin shacks I passed on my drive through Limpopo, the wealth hadn't trickled down to everyone. With nearly 25 percent unemployment and a history of violence, it was no wonder crime was high.

Despite Mmadithapelo's warning about men in the bushes, I did pull over to take a few photographs of the majestic Waterberg, a range of mountains that loomed ahead of me, sharper and starker than the Appalachians, more black and white than green. As I drove between them, there was one spectacular view after another—like a scene from *Lord of the Rings*, I thought, though with no town for a few hours, I felt like the Hobbit who complained about the shortage of snacks along the way. I felt slightly anxious by the time I finally found a restaurant, and the waitress said they were done serving lunch. I had a wallet full of Rand and two credit cards, so there was no chance I would experience real hunger, but observing my panic at one delayed meal was humbling.

Of all the things I was learning about climate change, the one that really hit me in the gut, so to speak, was its predicted effect on food supplies. The recent drought in the United States had already driven up the global price of maize, a staple for many Africans, though it was less drought resistant than indigenous crops like sorghum and millet. Like potatoes, maize had originated in the Americas and been spread around the world by European colonialism. I thought again of Ireland's early nineteenth-century dependence on potatoes—allegedly introduced to Ireland by an Englishman—and the human cost of that crop's failure.

I had grown up hearing about the English landlords who exported food during the Great Hunger and the Protestant churches that only gave aid to those who converted, which the Irish disparagingly referred to as "taking the soup." I'd read about the stingy relief efforts of the British government, often justified by the assertion that God was clearly punishing the Irish. I'd read that Queen Victoria—who called her Irish subjects "a terrible people"—only donated £2,000 to famine relief herself, and that when the Ottoman sultan offered to give £10,000, he was told he should only give £1,000 so as not to upstage the queen.

More recent writing about the famine had also included stories of generosity and compassion. In addition to the sultan, aid was sent by the Choctaw Nation, who remembered their own hunger sixteen years earlier when they were forced off their Tennessee land at gunpoint and driven west across the Mississippi as part of the deadly winter march known as the "Trail of Tears." I'd known that Quakers had run soup kitchens during the Hunger—a fact that had softened the blow for my mother when I joined a religion begun in England—but there were also many poorer English people who gave aid that was generous for their means. Even so, the aid was not sustained through the five-year crisis, so the overall picture was still grim. Some now argued that a million and a half had died during the famine, 50 percent more than the million I'd heard of when I studied in Dublin thirty years earlier.

Driving past the green farms and corrugated tin shacks of Limpopo Province, I wondered what made some people more compassionate than others. The Choctaw had faced famine themselves, and the English Quakers had been persecuted for their beliefs in the early decades of their faith. In South Africa, the whites who had been most courageous in opposing apartheid had been disproportionately Jewish, people who knew all too well the dangers of racism. Perhaps a history of being vulnerable made it easier (though not automatic) to feel connected to other people's suffering, I mused.

Given the most common images of Africans—from machete-wielding warlords to helpless children advertising some nongovernmental organization—I knew most Americans had a hard time feeling connected to Africans. I remembered several weeks earlier back in Philadelphia, I had told an acquaintance that I was going to visit my best friend from Botswana. "Oh, is she still there?" the woman had asked.

"Yes, she's still there," I replied. "That's where she's from."

It had taken an awkward number of seconds for this nice, liberal white woman to grasp that my best friend in Africa was African. I wondered how this inability to imagine Africans as potential friends would impact the way people in the West would respond to climate change in places like Limpopo.

In preparation for my trip, I had watched a video by Greenpeace Africa called *The Weather Gods*, which predicted that 180 million people in Sub-Saharan Africa could die in the twenty-first century as a result of climate change, from effects like famine, water shortages, and conflict over food and water. The statistic, which was based on a 2007 United Nations Food and Agriculture study, had shocked me. I could hardly wrap my mind around it. *A hundred and eighty million.* That was thirty Holocausts, 120 Irish Potato Famines. Even if the number was inflated—a worst-case scenario, double or triple what actually unfolded—it was still unimaginable.

The more tin settlements I passed, the easier it was to imagine.

A few hundred miles south of Dumela Lodge, where I'd chatted with David and Zazi about the plight of farmers in Botswana and the United States, I had a similar conversation, this time with white South Africans in a slightly more glamorous bush lodge just outside the small Limpopo town of Thabazimbi (which means mountain of iron). I had left my plans loose, wanting room for spontaneity on one of the only nights I wasn't going to be hosted by friends, but as the sun sank behind a mountain ridge, I searched nervously for a place to stay. I sighed with relief when I drove through the high gates of the Thaba 'Nkwe Bush Lodge, and the woman at the desk said they had a vacancy.

The lodge had a lofty thatched roof with a larger pool and a better Internet connection than Dumela Lodge. Instead of platform tents, there were little chalets with square thatched tops, sliding glass doors, and small kitchenettes. They seemed perfect for tourists who visited in warmer months hoping to see lion, rhino, and leopard at nearby game parks. I imagined how fun it would be to come back some day with Megan, Luke, and Tom, though if truth be told, I was less comfortable here than I'd been at the lower-security Botswana lodge, partly because I suspected the formidable fence around Thaba Nkwe was there to keep out the people in the tin shacks down the road, more than the leopards. Maybe it was an unfair stereotype, but from what I'd read about rural Afrikaners, I suspected the people who owned this place were armed to the teeth, which I found both reassuring and disquieting at the same time.

After putting my bag in my chalet, I walked the stone path to the main building, which included a sit-down restaurant and a bar that resembled an indoor rondavel with its own thatched roof. I claimed a stool at the bar and asked the young bartender if there was anything particularly South African I should try on their menu. He suggested spicy peri-peri chicken livers, which I ordered along with a beer.

The other bar stools were occupied by men speaking Afrikaans, which was now one of South Africa's eleven official languages. I couldn't help recognizing the word "America" sprinkled through their conversation, which passed across me as I sipped my lager. Feeling nosey, I asked in English what they were talking about, and a man in his sixties explained that they were talking about climate change. Turning to me, he launched into the same litany of complaints about the weather I had heard from Batswana: "The rain is unpredictable. The winter isn't cold enough to kill the pests. The crop yields have been terrible."

I said I'd just come from Botswana where people were saying the same exact things. The men on both sides of me nodded. "Water is a huge issue there," I added, curious to see if they were concerned about that, too.

It turned out the younger man to my right worked for a water purification company. Looking into his beer, he said that the coming water shortages in South Africa would be made worse by the fact that so much water had already been polluted from nearly 150 years of mining a range of minerals.

"It's hard to get uranium out of the water," he noted dryly. "All you can do is really, really water it down."

During my week in South Africa, I continued to hear about climate change and water scarcity, but I also met people devoted to addressing these issues. Given the country's brutal history, I found it particularly encouraging to see people working across racial lines. My first morning in Johannesburg, I visited Makoma Lekalakala, a strong-looking middle-aged woman who had cut her activist teeth during the struggle against apartheid. An organizer for Earthlife Africa who did both direct action and community education, Lekalakala was especially concerned with the effect of climate change on women, the family caregivers who bore the brunt of water shortages and higher food prices.

Empowering women to make government accountable to them was one of her passions. So was connecting issues, which Lekalakala referred to several times as "linkages." She first began to see the link between justice and the environment during apartheid when, as part of the growing trade union movement, she had learned about Thor Chemicals, a British company whose South African workers were developing severe mercury poisoning. Turned out the company, which reprocessed toxic waste from other countries including the United States, was contaminating local water as well as workers. Even forty miles downstream, near the coastal city of Durban, mercury levels in the water were twenty times the US limit, even higher in the rural areas closer to the plant, where people bathed and grazed their cattle.

At the time, Lekalakala explained, people like her thought this was just part of how the apartheid government operated and that getting a black president would solve such problems. Today, she realized, that a black president was not enough.

"Industries are actually the ones making decisions in this country," she explained. "They have the upper hand in government. The people don't have a voice." For example, she said that it had been energy-intensive industries that had pushed for South Africa to build two of the largest coal-powered stations in the world. One was still under construction not far from the route I had just traveled through Limpopo Province.

"The local people, farmers who know the area very well, know there are going to be water shortages if these plants are built," explained Lekalakala. "But business doesn't care about people's rights. Most of those who are preparing the environmental impact statements are on the side of industry."

An hour later, in the pleasant, light-filled offices of Greenpeace Africa, Melita Steele expounded on the increased competition for water expected as a result of the coal plants.

"You need water throughout the process of coal production—from the coal mining to the washing to the dust suppression," she began. "But then you also need water for the power station to operate, including both cooling and sulfur reduction. Despite the latest technology, these stations will use a lot of water because of their size," she explained.

A younger South African who had studied environmental science, Steele agreed with Lekalakala that the surrounding communities would be the ones to suffer and that profit was part of the problem. Eskom, South Africa's electricity monopoly, was owned by the government, and the ANC—the ruling party—was financially benefiting from the construction of the two plants. Just the previous week, she said, it had come out that ANC contractors had gotten the lucrative contracts to build both boilers. The tens of billions of dollars that South Africa was investing in these plants could have been put into renewable energy, she argued, like solar and wind, which used less water, released less carbon, and had fewer health impacts.

After Melita Steele, I spoke to Greenpeace communications director, Fiona Musana, who told me more about how Greenpeace Africa was tackling these problems. "Dialogue is very important to us," she said, tracing this priority to the African concept of *ubuntu* (often translated as "I am because we are").

A tall, elegant woman originally from Uganda, Musana asserted that while Greenpeace challenged powerful institutions around the world—most famously with dramatic tactics like dropping banners from tall buildings—in Africa, where they were relatively new, part of their organizing strength came from this indigenous belief in people's deep interconnectedness. She emphasized the importance of establishing a dialog with different groups, like the trade unions who would benefit from the development of green technology but who wouldn't hear that message from those profiting from coal.

"What we've tried to do since the office was launched in November 2008," said Musana, "is to really try to speak with people and follow very much in the tradition of this continent, the *ubuntu* spirit."

In one video interview where Nelson Mandela was asked to explain what *ubuntu* meant, he replied, "In the old days, when we were young, a traveler through our country would stop at the village, and he didn't have to ask for food or for water. Once he stops, the people give him food, entertain him." He went on to explain that *ubuntu* did not mean neglecting oneself but taking care of oneself in a way that was also good for the community. I thought of it as recognizing our deep connection to other people, reflecting the same cultural roots as the proverb, "A person is a person because of other people," which I learned existed in some other southern African languages as well as Setswana.

Despite the problems of contemporary South Africa, I could still feel the *ubuntu* spirit. At Earthlife Africa, Makoma Lekalakala had sent a woman to hail me a taxi, not by making a phone call or flagging someone down, but by walking me around an area of parked taxis until she found the particular guy whom she knew would get me safely to the Greenpeace office at a fair price. During a two-day side trip to visit

Kumi's family in Durban, he had noticed I was cold and gave me a second blanket, which I realized in the morning had been the one from his bed. The next day, one of his friends offered to bring me shopping in an Indian neighborhood while another offered to go out and get us a special kind of curry.

In the course of my week in South Africa, I experienced such hospitality from people of every racial group. I was particularly touched by it in Soweto, the southwestern townships near Johannesburg famous for the 1976 uprising in which at least 176 students were shot and killed for protesting the imposition of the Afrikaans language. My guide Laureen—a white woman who used to teach there—told me that most white South Africans were too scared to go near the place, though Soweto had changed a lot in the thirty-six years since the uprising. For starters, much of the housing had improved. Most numerous were the rows of small cinder block homes, now fed by electrical lines, though there were also more upscale homes with two-car garages.

When we stopped outside Mandela's former home, which had been made into a small museum, a man approached us to sell his wares. After all the warnings about crime, I could feel my hand tighten around my purse, but Laureen looked warmly at his tiny bottles of sand designs and said, "What have you got here? Oh they are so intricate! You made these yourself?" I felt my hand relax.

He proudly told us about his art as we studied the glass bottles, half the length of my hand. I couldn't imagine how he'd arranged the sand into words on one side and dancing African figures on the other, with a colored design that encircled the bottleneck. I pulled out my wallet and bought one for Tom that said, "Love from Africa."

A single mother herself, Laureen wanted to "support the local economy" by getting a car wash when a man offered her one for a few Rand. Near the memorial for Hector Pieterson, the first student killed during the Soweto Uprising, there stood tables of African crafts, their makers smiling broadly to attract the business of the few tourists. Following Laureen's example, I bought three braided metal bracelets for friends, a blue beaded one for Megan, and a small wooden carving for Luke, sure that my money was needed here more than at the expensive airport gift shops.

Noticing that my lips were dry from the winter weather, Laureen ducked into a shop and bought me some Vaseline. I mentioned how moved I was by her care and my experience of *ubuntu* in South Africa. She affirmed my observation but added wryly, "We are very nice to tourists, just not to each other."

Indeed the evidence of South Africa's high crime rate was everywhere. Part of the reason I was carefully led to the right taxi driver was to make sure I was safe. The Earthlife Africa office kept the toilet paper hidden so it wouldn't be stolen. I knew this was a legacy of the violence and gross inequalities of apartheid, but I was still taken aback when Laureen left me alone at a friend's Johannesburg apartment and said, "Lock the door and don't answer for anyone, no matter what they say." Locking the door behind her required three different keys.

Although this apartment was arguably not in the greatest neighborhood, I'd also been struck by the number of keys and locks in the more upscale home I'd stayed in my first two nights in South Africa. I couldn't help remembering Gandhi saying something about feeling joy when he no longer owned anything that someone else might want to steal because he didn't need to protect himself anymore. I wasn't ready to go that far—and certainly didn't blame my friends for being cautious—but seeing the extreme inequality in South Africa confirmed my growing sense that such a wide gap between rich and poor wasn't really good for anyone.

One of my favorite anecdotes about Nelson Mandela was about his simplicity. Instead of building the sort of extravagant palace that stereotypically corrupt African leaders were known for, he had built himself a replica of the pleasant but unostentatious bungalow where he'd stayed during his final months of imprisonment. He said he was comfortable there. Not everyone had embraced Mandela's example. The current president, Jacob Zuma, was said to have renovated his private home with an extraordinary $22,000,000 of public money.

Even more shocking to me was what I had learned from Melita Steele, that the African National Congress as a political party now owned an investment company that profited from the very policies that were fueling climate change. South Africa was in the process of establishing private funding for more renewable energy, but many felt it wasn't enough of a priority, given the country's wind and solar potential. More than one person had told me that the greatest obstacle to renewable energy was the fact that politicians were in bed with the fossil fuel companies—just like in the United States.

As an outsider, I didn't want to be too critical. The ANC had accomplished a tremendous amount against incredible odds. They had changed more than most Westerners predicted, more than most people dared to change in a lifetime. I hoped to have a fraction of their courage and impact. At the same time, the ANC illustrated how hard it was to make real change when the larger systems and incentives stayed in place. The profit motive that had led Europeans to colonize Africa to begin with was still driving the exploitation of resources without regard to the land or the people who lived on it, even if the faces of those who profited were now more racially diverse.

On my last full day in Johannesburg, I attended a National Women's Day panel that included Mary Robinson, the former President of Ireland and honorary head of Oxfam. I had heard her speak once before, years ago with my mother on the Main Line. Now, she was speaking at a business school, and the lecture hall was full of well-dressed young Africans. Robinson talked about Ireland's economic boom, often referred to as the Celtic Tiger, which began in the mid-1990s and collapsed during the global recession of 2008.

"It was such a boom time. Everyone wanted a higher and higher salary," she said in an Irish accent that sounded creamier than my relatives' rough brogue.

The Irish started to lose their culture's version of *ubuntu*, which Robinson said was called *meitheal* in Irish, a term I'd never heard before. A traditional example of the *meitheal* spirit was when all the men of a rural community gathered to harvest each other's fields in turn, and the women brought tea, bread, and jam. "If a neighbor was sick, his field would be done," she explained. It sounded like traditional Botswana, except that in Africa it was often women who tended the fields.

Robinson asserted that in Ireland prosperity had eroded the old ways, though when the economy crashed, people went back to their traditional communal spirit. Using the Irish experience as a warning, she urged the ambitious young African business students not to forget, "Your success is owed to the community."

The last leg of my trip was to Cape Town, where I planned to visit Robben Island. The notorious prison was now a guidebook destination with former political prisoners conducting educational tours. I thought it would be an inspirational way to spend the afternoon of my fiftieth birthday while my host Fiona was at work.

When I was still living at Pendle Hill in the fall of 1993, Tom and I had become friends with Fiona, an English Quaker (not to be confused with the Fiona who worked for Greenpeace). Fiona had married a South African named Stanley, who was originally from Limpopo Province. They lived in Cape Town with Stanley's two children in a three-bedroom home—a little larger than our old home, but smaller than our new one—with a spectacular view of Table Mountain just over their fence. When Fiona had turned up in Philadelphia right as I was planning my trip, it felt destined that I should go visit them. In the end, I'd decided to spend my fiftieth birthday there.

While Fiona was at work, Stanley offered to drive me around Khayelitsha, a township of 1.2 million people. I'd wanted to get closer to the corrugated tin shacks, to feel what those places were like, but as an outsider I was not sure how to do that in a way that felt respectful to the people who lived there. Stanley knew the area well enough to show me around and bring me to the maternal and child nutrition program where Fiona used to work, where I could buy a few more handmade gifts from its employment program to bring back home. We had to drive the long way because there was a riot at one end of the township that morning, which Stanley said was not uncommon.

Khayelitsha was an endless quilt of tin and poverty. Along the road, I counted thirty-three blue porta-potties, which Stanley said were installed by the local government. The city had also built some flush toilets in an area of Khayelitsha called Makhaza but with no walls around them, outraging the community. The city council said people in Makhaza—a huge percentage of whom were unemployed—should build the walls themselves, leading to a protracted struggle that newspapers referred to as "the toilet wars" until the South African Human Rights Commission ruled in the residents' favor. Along the road, men sold rows of wooden doghouses that looked sturdier than the nearby shacks. Above it all hung the surreally beautiful mountains of the Cape topped with a teal-blue sky.

After Khayelitsha, Stanley delivered me to the Cape Town docks where I discovered that the afternoon ferry to Robben Island had been cancelled due to high winds. I walked along the waterfront, past a jewelry store with diamonds in the window, a white Ferris wheel, and a mall full of luxury stores—a world away from Khayelitsha, though with the same shockingly beautiful Cape Town sky. This was the very port the Dutch East India Company had established in 1652 to resupply its trading ships on the long, lucrative trip from Europe to the East, the spot where South Africa's colonial history had begun. Now it was a tourist destination, described by one website as "an African success story," a model of development.

Fiona was planning a birthday dinner of Cape Malay food, a local specialty. In the meantime, I bought myself a decaf latte, disappointed that after a seamless trip, my plan to go to Robben Island had fallen through. I had been looking for some grand finale, something to infuse this next part of my life with meaning, some inspiration to carry me home to my family and a more committed life. What had I imagined, peering into Mandela's old cell and imbibing some remnant of his spirit? Feeling the chilling winds off Table Bay and suddenly understanding where courage came from? Catching some, like a sail in the wind?

Throughout my trip I'd received many visceral reminders of the courage of the South Africans who had fought apartheid. Mr. Rahube, my host in Bobonong, had spent ten years on Robben Island. In Durban, Kumi showed me where he'd led his first march, at age fifteen, and took me to the grave of his best friend, Lenny Naidu, who was brutally killed by a covert security unit in 1988. In Johannesburg, I'd visited the Apartheid Museum and wandered alone among exhibits that brought the history to life, including a mass of nooses hanging from the ceiling, a reminder of those who were executed for resisting the regime.

Not everyone had shown such courage. I understood those who had quietly criticized the system but never risked much to oppose it. I wasn't sure what I was willing to risk today for a more just and sustainable economy, but I knew I was called to ask the question after this trip. It occurred to me that seeing Khayelitsha might have been the perfect outing after all for a birthday that seemed to mark a turning point. Feeling connected to the places in the world where people were most vulnerable felt more likely to inspire me than stepping into an historical exhibit.

I remembered a story from *The Things They Carried* by Tim O'Brien. The narrator of O'Brien's semi-autobiographical fiction reflected on a turning point in his life, the moment when he tried to escape to Canada to dodge the Vietnam War, which he thought was wrong. In that moment, when the Canadian shore was in sight, fear held him back, to his eternal shame and regret. Years later, scarred by the war, he mused that courage wasn't something you could save up and use when you needed it; it was more like a muscle that you developed by using it. Perhaps that was part of the purpose of this trip, I thought, to exercise my courage muscles.

People in Earth Quaker Action Team often talked about stepping out of our comfort zones, doing new things, and how empowering that could be. At one party, Carolyn had played the piano just to move past her fear of playing in public. Another day at a general meeting, she talked about civil disobedience as something that made her uncomfortable, but then explained, "When I think about climate change and all the suffering that it will cause across the planet, the discomfort of getting arrested or having my hands in handcuffs seems very slight. So I'm willing to do something uncomfortable for that reason."

I'd been thinking that I might be ready to commit civil disobedience when I got home. It felt like the next needed step, a nonviolent way of challenging the corporations that were profiting from the earth's destruction. While my experiences of *ubuntu* in South Africa had inspired me to be more generous in my own life, I knew for certain now that individual simplicity and generosity were not enough to transform a system that fostered both economic inequality and environmental destruction. We needed new ways of thinking about development—ways that enabled the people in Khayelitsha to have access to electricity and dignified toilets without following the economic model that was causing water shortages in Bobonong and climate change everywhere. We needed models that made use of both modern technology and the communal wisdom of the Batswana and the Irish—and probably traditional cultures around the globe—models, like Transition Town, that encouraged our best natures rather than our greed.

Looking out at the water of Table Bay—water that encircled Robben Island and connected all the way north to Ireland and west to my own shores—I didn't know exactly what my place in this transition would be, but I knew that I wanted to use my gifts there. I wanted to keep stepping out of my comfort zone, in my political work and in the rest of my life, trusting that way would open, like a supermarket door that swings wide only when we walk toward it.

Chapter Fourteen:
Ordinary People

If the world is to be healed through human efforts, I am convinced it will be by ordinary people, people whose love for this life is even greater than their fear. People who can open to the web of life that called us into being.

—Joanna R. Macy

Despite all I had learned, coming home from Africa this time was not nearly as hard as coming home from the Peace Corps because now I had a support committee willing to sit through my slides—from the cattle on the dry Shashi River bed to the blue porta-potties of Khayelitsha. Tom, Megan, and Luke listened to my stories, and two local Quaker meetings hosted talks about my trip. Speaking at a rally against fracking on behalf of EQAT, I told a street full of people, the largest crowd I'd ever addressed, about the connection between our struggle and South Africa's.

I also wrote several articles, doing additional research on climate change in Africa—from the shrinking of Lakes Chad and Turkana to the innovative ways Africans were adapting, such as planting shade trees among their crops in the Sahel.

One article was about a group of South Africans who had mobilized to prevent fracking in the Karoo, an ecologically fragile desert northeast of Cape Town. Turned out a few South African farmers had visited Pennsylvania to see the effects of fracking and came home even more determined to keep the water-intensive process away from their drought-prone farmland. From my desk in Philadelphia, I skyped Jonathan Deal, the leader of the grassroots group Treasure the Karoo Action Group, who said that the ministry in charge of issuing extraction permits would directly profit from it. "It's like putting the fox in charge of the hen house," he said.

The public outcry against fracking had gotten the South African government to issue a moratorium on gas exploration, though it was lifted as I was doing the final edits on my article, forcing me to do a quick rewrite. Citizens were up against Shell, Deal explained, an international company with unlimited resources. And yet they hadn't given up. They were making a stand and a difference.

Back in Philadelphia, I watched a YouTube video of a multilingual and interracial rally against fracking in the tiny Karoo town of Nieu-Bethesda. Along with the farmers who owned the land, a South African landless people's group was challenging Shell. It made so much sense when you thought about it. Of course, the descendants of people who had been dispossessed relied on the same water as the descendants of the people who'd dispossessed them and had the same desire to protect it. Although I imagined the organizing dynamics were fraught, I found the story profoundly hopeful. It showed that, while the history of colonialism had created a situation where people bore the effects of climate change unevenly, the crisis might—just might—give people an incentive to write a new story together.

Climate change had certainly motivated a change in my own life. For years my work had felt disjointed—my University of the Arts and Pendle Hill classes were disconnected from each other and my volunteer projects, not to mention parenting. Now my life was starting to feel more integrated around the mission of keeping the planet habitable, for my children and for Mmadithapelo's. With others from Earth Quaker Action Team, I helped to organize a fall weekend training for people who would go on to organize their own actions for EQAT. The participants ranged in age from twenty to eighty, with varying levels of political experience. Six weeks later we held fifteen actions at PNC branches in five states plus the District of Columbia. The hope I found in such organizing work actually made it easier to make little personal sacrifices, like eating less meat and hanging our laundry on the line, something Tom had long advocated.

One day, a month after my return, I was rushing to get ready for an EQAT meeting when I realized a dilemma. There were clothes in the washer that I needed the next day, but if I took the time to hang them on the line, I would miss the train to the meeting. I had to use at least one, the car or the dryer, if I was going to make the meeting, which felt nonnegotiable. Whether it was in terms of eating less or using less fuel, I was now clear that no amount of personal conservation would ever save as much carbon as stopping mountaintop removal coal mining, so that was my priority.

I had knocked on doors for Barack Obama, when he first ran for president in 2008, and had even organized a town hall meeting for his campaign at a local Irish pub. By 2012, I understood we couldn't wait for a president to solve the climate crisis. My South African friends would have their work cut out for them holding their government to its democratic ideals. It was my job to do that here, in the country that so many around the world emulated and which had such a disproportionate effect on international climate negotiations. When I heard that 350.org was planning an enormous climate rally in Washington, DC for February 2013, I knew I'd be there and started lobbying the rest of the EQAT board to mobilize people in Philadelphia to go.

The First Nations—the indigenous people of Canada—had been at the forefront of the struggle against tar sands extraction, a process that like mountaintop removal and fracking contaminated a lot of water, endangering the health of nearby residents. The most economical route for tar sands export was the proposed Keystone XL pipeline, from Alberta, Canada, across the middle of the United States, to the refineries in the Gulf of Mexico, and then reportedly overseas. Communities along the pipeline's route were resisting. The mounting campaign had gotten my attention when I heard that NASA scientist Dr. James Hansen said it would mean "game over" for the planet if the tar sands were all burned, they contained that much carbon. In the past year, many groups had come together to stop the pipeline, which would be the focus of February's Forward on Climate March.

One day when Mmadithapelo called, I told her that, partly because of my trip, I planned to protest a pipeline that was intended to ship oil from Canada across the middle of the United States.

"That's crazy," she said. "Anyone can see that if you build a pipe all that long way it is going to leak somewhere." Indeed.

Unfortunately, the people who hoped to profit from the pipeline were having a hard time seeing how dangerous the extraction, the transportation, and the burning of the oil was—but ordinary people did. According to inside sources, the pipeline had been considered a "done deal" before the summer of 2011, but its approval became uncertain after more than twelve hundred people committed civil disobedience in front of the White House. Because it would cross an international border, President Obama had the authority to stop the project, and that's what activists were asking him to do.

Late in 2012, a few months after my return from Africa, I was talking on the phone with Daniel Hunter, an esteemed trainer and facilitator, who was doing a stint as a consultant with Earth Quaker Action Team. Daniel told me that, a few days before the national climate rally, a small group would be committing civil disobedience in front of the White House, though it wasn't public knowledge yet. He had told Joshua Kahn Russell, one of the action organizers, that he thought EQAT should be included as a faith-based group that was modeling bold, nonviolent direct action.

I had an immediate intuition that I would be part of the group to risk arrest at the White House, even though the plan was to invite high-profile people who could attract media attention. Despite my growing leadership in EQAT, I certainly wasn't in the same league as the head of the Sierra Club, which was going to sanction the first act of civil disobedience in its long history. Still, I knew in my gut that I was meant to be there and shared my interest with Daniel. With his encouragement, I also sent an e-mail to Bill McKibben, gently advocating for EQAT's involvement.

One night as I was putting on my pajamas, I told Tom about the action and asked how he'd feel about me getting arrested. After a moment's pause, he sat up in bed and said, "I support you whatever you feel called to do . . . as long as you don't turn violent." I smiled and leaned over the bed to give him a kiss of reassurance.

Way did open, and Earth Quaker Action Team was invited to send a representative to the action, which would be on Ash Wednesday at the White House, though the details were still not public. The board approved sending me to risk arrest, which Ingrid pointed out made sense, not just because I was eager to do it and had experience talking to the media, but also because I had a wider reputation as a Quaker leader and was the person who had been encouraging EQAT to connect with the national climate movement, through the "connect the dots" photo and now the Forward on Climate Rally. We agreed that I would travel with Ingrid and another EQAT leader, Amy Ward Brimmer, who would come both to support me and to network with other organizations.

A small group in EQAT had been meeting to talk about how spiritual practices might ground our social action, which got me thinking about fasting as a way to prepare for what I already suspected would only be my first experience of civil disobedience. The first time I'd heard fasting mentioned in EQAT had been at a daylong strategy retreat a few months earlier. About twenty people had gathered to brainstorm our plans for the next nine months, thinking of ways we could be bolder and more effective. Someone had mentioned fasting. Over the break, Zack and I had loitered on the edge of the large, sunlit room near the package of chocolate chip cookies, commiserating about how much we hated the idea of fasting.

"I'd much rather protest naked than fast," I'd joked, though it really wasn't true.

"Me, too!" laughed Zack, reaching for another cookie.

"But if we're ever going to protest naked, maybe I should fast first to lose some weight," I'd said. We were both still laughing when we were called back from the break and put into small groups for deeper discussion. Of course, I ended up in the group that was gung ho about fasting.

"To be bold enough to make the kind of changes our society needs, we must increase our capacity for suffering," Walter had said earnestly. I'd found this both true and pretty annoying.

For Gandhi, demonstrating a willingness to suffer was an important part of what made nonviolence effective. He didn't commit civil disobedience and then run like hell when the police showed up. He faced the consequences. His public fasts were designed both for self-purification and to demonstrate the lengths he would go for justice, which was key to building a movement powerful enough to dislodge the British Empire. In Ireland, too, fasting was a practice with both religious and political roots. In pre-Christian Ireland, I'd read, a person who felt aggrieved could sit down on the offending person's door-step and refuse to eat, heaping bad luck upon the offender unless he redressed the grievance or engaged in a counter-fast.

During the strategy retreat, I noticed my internal resistance to the idea of fasting and my incredulity when Kaz said that he could go two weeks without eating—that was just how he was wired. That was *not* how I was wired.

I'd heard recently that the descendants of famine survivors were more likely to have weight issues than other people. When I'd googled that, I found conflicting explanations. Some websites said it was because those who stored fat easily had more energy to draw from when times got tough, giving them a survival edge. Others said that the experience of famine itself changed one physiologically, and not only the individual but the genes one passed on to descendants, so they became better at storing fat, too.

I was fascinated by the possibility that my weight struggles might be related to something that had happened to my ancestors a century and a half ago. That sounded much more interesting than just being middle-aged. But the theory also felt like a metaphor for the American Dream. In a country where many people's ancestors had fled or experienced deprivation, of course it was hard to choose to consume less, though that was what we needed to do to protect our own children, not to mention the seventh generation. Excess was programmed into us, but it was no longer adaptive.

Now as I contemplated my first act of civil disobedience, I decided to give fasting a try. With the support of a few people in the spiritual practices group, I'd just do a day at a time, each Wednesday for the month before the action. The first day, I eyed the gummy bear vitamins at 7:00 a.m. and wondered if eating a handful would be cheating. I made it through that day and then the following Wednesday, though grumpily. Since I was due for my first colonoscopy—a joy of turning fifty—I scheduled my fasting test prep for the third Wednesday, which felt a little devious, but as a mother I was used to multitasking. I didn't feel all mystical or purified skipping solid food, but there still seemed to be something important about testing my resolve to make change. It was another little step.

One member of the spiritual practices group, Ann Yasuhara, told me how much she admired Quaker Alice Paul, a women's suffrage leader. I had seen the film *Iron Jawed Angels* at George's house a year earlier and knew that Paul and others had been arrested at the White House, but now I wanted to know the details, in case I had the chance to position myself where they had stood. A retired math professor who had climbed a West Virginia mountain on her seventy-ninth birthday a year earlier to protest mountaintop removal, Ann took it upon herself to reread *Alice Paul and the American Suffrage Campaign,* looking for the exact location for me.

I knew Alice Paul had had it much rougher than I would. When she went on hunger strike in 1917 to protest the deplorable conditions in the prison that held the suffragists, she was force-fed raw eggs, which shocked the public so much it arguably helped push Woodrow Wilson into signing the Nineteenth Amendment, securing women's right to vote. In contrast, I expected to be released within a few hours, though you never knew for sure how these things would go. Thinking about Alice Paul reminded me of George's point, that nonviolent direct action had a history of leading to change, though most of us hadn't learned those stories in school.

Leading up to the action, I also asked for people to pray for me—a request that had a comic flavor since the exact date and location of the civil disobedience were still closely guarded secrets. Kathy, a member of my meeting who had been on my support committee when I went to southern Africa, agreed to collect the names of those who wanted an e-mail notification when the day came, so they could hold me in prayer. Again, I felt connected to something larger than myself.

Walking with Deb in the wintry woods, I shared my excitement and my sense that the White House action was a next step in the journey she had been witnessing for over a year.

"Well, it's a good thing we are all called in different ways," she said laughing. "Because there is no part of it that sounds fun to me."

A year earlier, I might have worried what my more conservative friends or in-laws would think of my breaking the law, but now I was feeling comfortable with the prospect of being "creatively maladjusted," as King had put it. Instead, I was worried that I wasn't famous enough for the list of people that were part of the Ash Wednesday action, many of them founders or heads of organizations. I was asked to write up my bio for the press release and spent longer than necessary fussing over the wording. Belonging to a religion and an organization that didn't have the kind of titles recognized by the wider world, I settled for the generic word "leader," though I hesitated to claim it until Daniel and Ingrid assured me it was true.

"Damn right, you're a leader!" said Ingrid, which made me smile.

The night before leaving for DC, I decided to skip EQAT's monthly general meeting and spend the time with Tom, Megan, and Luke, who took me to a local Mexican restaurant for a vegetarian chimichanga. The next day I would practice my press talking points during the three-hour drive with Amy and Ingrid, and then head to a night-before training with the other action participants. I had intended to take some quiet reflective time during the day, but that got short shrift between checking e-mail, drafting an article on the action, and packing. I picked out a grey pair of pants and dug out my best leather gloves. I packed my brand new pair of reading glasses, a concession to turning fifty, as well as my friend Daniel Hunter's new book *Strategy and Soul* about a nonviolent direct action campaign against casinos in Philadelphia.

After a hectic afternoon and evening, I realized at 9:00 p.m. that I was feeling surprisingly calm. I went on my computer to check e-mail one last time before bed and found a few messages from EQAT members, telling me that they had prayed for me during a final period of silence at the meeting I'd missed.

"Could you feel it?" they asked. Yes, I actually could.

On the morning of the action, I woke up, heart racing, and grabbed my iPhone in the dark to check the time. It was 3:00 a.m., and I was alone in the basement guest room of Ingrid's mother's house, just outside Washington, DC.

"Damn it," I thought, "all the people who are supposed to be praying for me are asleep."

And then I laughed out loud in the dark. Just over a year earlier, I had been waking up at 3:00 a.m. to stare at the ceiling fan in despair. Now I was awake with excitement. I turned on the small bedside lamp and reached for the card Tom had selected for the occasion. On the front was a photo of a polar bear leaping from one ice floe to the next, its front paws stretched out expectantly in midair—no longer on solid ground, but not quite landed on the next floe yet. Inside, the card, Tom, Megan, and Luke had each written me a similar note, which I reread in the dim light.

"I'm happy you care this much about something that will affect the future of us all," sixteen-year-old Megan had written. "Good luck!" I smiled—imagining her brown eyes, flaming red hair, and porcelain face—and turned off the light again.

As the sun rose over suburban Maryland, I dressed in layers for the February cold and put on a little makeup, just in case I got the chance to speak into a TV camera. After a breakfast of scrambled eggs, Ingrid and I shared a few minutes of silent worship in her mother's living room, then headed downtown to meet up with Amy before joining the press junket in Lafayette Square.

"I put on enough mascara so that people will know I'm not Amish," I said to Reverend Jim Antal a few hours later, as TV reporters honed in on civil rights icon Julian Bond and Sierra Club head Michael Brune.

Jim laughed loudly. In a career devoted to peace and justice, he had worked with Quakers enough to know we were not the bonnet-wearing Amish with whom we were often confused. For his part, Jim was wearing a clerical collar and a red baseball cap. I looked across Lafayette Square at the north side of the White House, wondering where Alice Paul had been arrested for demanding the vote for women nearly a century earlier. Ann hadn't found the exact spot, though I did find a photograph of the suffragists standing in the same area where I would be standing soon. I'd made it my Facebook banner image.

Over the last century, the DC Park Police had gotten used to White House protests. It was a different story along the frontlines of extreme extraction. In Texas, where the southern leg of the pipeline was already under construction, two Texas natives had been pepper-sprayed and tasered repeatedly for sitting down in the pipeline's path. I was glad that some of the forty-eight in our group were from those communities. One man who was from Texas said with a laugh, "I can't believe how polite the police are here."

Maria Gunnoe—whom I'd met a few months earlier at a DC rally to end mountaintop removal in Appalachia—had received death threats in her native West Virginia, where a recent action had led to twenty arrests. I'd heard from a young woman who'd been there that the police had beaten up some of the men. The arrested women were denied sanitary supplies during the week they spent in a West Virginia jail, with bail set at $25,000 each. Like Alice Paul and my South African friends, the people I was getting to know from Appalachia were models of courage. It didn't seem fair that our White House action would get more media coverage than theirs.

After a few speeches, including Jim Antal's words about Ash Wednesday, our band of forty-eight walked slowly toward the White House gate, reporters jostling as we went. Joshua was handing out Clif Bars to tide us over for the hours it would take to process us through the DC Park Police system. Those who would be standing in back along the wrought iron fence were given plastic handcuffs, as the front row found their spots on the sidewalk. I snapped one end of my handcuff around the fence, the other around my left leather glove, and waited.

After giving us three warnings over a megaphone, the police came first for actress Daryl Hannah, who stood up and allowed her hands to be stretched behind her blue jacket and snapped into cuffs, her long blond hair and red scarf blowing gently in the breeze, while photographers snapped wildly. We'd been told they would arrest us by gender, so I felt my heart quicken, knowing my turn was coming soon. I pulled off my leather gloves with my free hand and stuffed them into my pocket, thinking that I'd be hot wearing them inside the police van and station. I wondered how long I'd have both hands constrained once I was arrested and how long I'd have to wait for a bathroom, a concern that had prompted me to cut back on coffee and water that morning. In a moment of mild panic about missing lunch, I pulled out the chocolate chip Clif Bar I'd been given, ripped open the wrapping, and gulped it down.

The police were respectful when they came for me, announcing that I was under arrest and clipping off my handcuffs with giant shears.

"Put your hands behind your back, please," said a policeman who slid on new plastic handcuffs, tightening each side so that my wrists crossed at my tailbone. Then he led me into what was now a line of women waiting to enter a small white tent, which looked like it could be for gifts at a wedding. To my left stood the press, to my right the crowd of cheering supporters who had been moved behind a barrier.

A female officer approached and asked if I had my ID. I gave her permission to fish my driver's license out of my pocket, and she put it in a gallon Ziploc bag along with my leather gloves and the No KXL pin I'd worn on my coat. As per instructions, I had left everything else at home, even my wedding ring, to cut down on the number of things the police needed to process, though today they didn't seem to be bothering with anyone's jewelry.

After moving slowly through the tent, where two policemen sat taking names and making sure they matched our IDs, I was steered to a police van where four other women were already squeezed onto a metal bench, their hands awkwardly behind them. There was a thin metal wall down the middle of the van, separating us from the women lined against the other side, whose muffled voices we could hear dimly through the metal.

If this had been an EQAT action, there would have been singing— "This Little Light of Mine" or "We Are a Gentle, Angry People." Although my singing voice had been gradually getting stronger, I wasn't yet confident enough to start a song with a group that didn't seem so inclined. Instead I played the role of facilitator, introducing myself and asking my van-mates where they were from. There was a middle-aged college professor, a college student, a young woman working to stop a coal plant in North Carolina, a blond rancher in a red Nebraska jacket and spats. Some had committed civil disobedience before; some had not. By the time we reached the Anacostia Police Station, we'd agreed that the movement needed more women in leadership positions. The men in ties outnumbered us and had given most of the speeches.

At the station, we joined the rest of the women in a windowless concrete room that felt like a two-car garage, except for the concrete steps where we sat, exchanging stories as the police processed us slowly one by one. I sat next to a representative of the Michigan National Association for the Advancement of Colored People (NAACP) for about an hour, talking about the fact that climate change would disproportionately affect people of color, until it was my turn to stand in the slow-moving line with my hands still behind my back. When the last of the women were standing, the first van of men arrived and took our places in the concrete room. We greeted them through a wire fence, everyone smiling, in good spirits.

When my handcuffs were finally clipped off, I rubbed my right thumb, which had become numb from my wrists being constrained, and took a seat before an officer who held my driver's license and confirmed my identity. In a brief moment of panic, I realized that my license had the address of my old row house, even though I'd officially changed it with the state of Pennsylvania a year earlier. The policeman behind the desk didn't care. He gave me a receipt for my $100 fine and pointed me toward the door.

Compared to the windowless prison, the sky seemed bright, even though it was overcast, threatening rain. Swinging my arms and wiggling my thumb, I walked across the dried grass and past a few police cars to join a small welcome committee on the sidewalk. Amy and Ingrid planted huge kisses on each of my cheeks, and Joshua gave me a hug and another Clif Bar.

Although my thumb stayed numb for another week, the most painful part of the whole experience was realizing the next morning that every photo of Daryl Hannah's arrest—starting with *The New York Times*—had caught me chewing my chocolate chip Clif Bar in the background. Aside from wounding my vanity, the photo proved that three weeks of fasting hadn't been enough to lick my own appetites, which would clearly be an ongoing struggle. When my college friend Maureen called and I told her about the photo, she googled it as we spoke and laughed so hard I was tempted to hang up on her.

"I'm proud of you," she said when she stopped laughing, which meant more to me than the photo.

I returned to Philadelphia for Valentine's Day lunch with Tom and a few days at home before we rode back to DC with Megan and members of both our congregations on one of the buses EQAT had rented for Saturday's Forward on Climate Rally. There was not going to be civil disobedience that day, but George argued that a huge showing on Saturday made my arrest the previous Wednesday more effective than it would have been if we had just been forty-eight people disconnected from an ongoing campaign and a growing movement.

"We know from history that we are best able to overcome powerful entrenched interests when we combine mass numbers of people taking a stand—like the 1963 March on Washington—along with smaller numbers of trained nonviolent activists willing to demonstrate the seriousness of their cause by taking bigger risks—like those who sat down at segregated lunch counters in the South," he explained when I interviewed him for an article about why our small direct action group was mobilizing for this large march.

The groundbreaking 1963 march had brought together people from the frontlines of the civil rights struggle, those working on voting rights alongside those fighting for economic justice. Quaker visionary Bayard Rustin had been the lead organizer of the event, which brought well over 200,000 people to the mall, more than anyone had predicted. Less than a year later, President Johnson signed the Civil Rights Act, arguably in response to the people power the march conveyed.

In the decades since, big marches had become commonplace in Washington, though none had yet been organized around climate change. Although Earth Quaker Action Team was wary of attending events that weren't strategic or directly about our issue—PNC Bank's financing of mountaintop removal coal mining—we'd decided that the Forward on Climate Rally was worth it, not only because it was tied to the civil disobedience I was part of, but also because it was part of the same campaign that had gotten over twelve hundred people arrested more than a year earlier, stalling the pipeline's approval. EQAT had rented two buses to bring people to the march, but so many had signed up, we'd had to keep adding buses until we had six, each with two EQAT members designated to lead the singing and collect e-mail addresses in the hope of recruiting people to our campaign.

"When we talk about the threat—the fossil fuel industry—we tend to make it very large," said George, stretching out his long arms, "and we are very small. We need to have the experience of being the many."

When we arrived at the mall, I found other people I knew in the crowd of 40,000—a guy who'd been in the Peace Corps with me in Bobonong, a man from the first Quaker meeting I'd attended twenty years earlier, and a Quaker I knew from Wisconsin. In the course of the day, I also ran into two of the people I'd been arrested with four days earlier: Reverend Lennox Yearwood, Jr. of the Hip Hop Caucus and Cherri Foytlin, the Louisiana mother of six who had walked to DC to protest the lax response to the BP oil spill. Making these connections in such a huge crowd felt surprisingly natural, the threads of my life weaving together into a stronger cord.

We all stood in the bitter wind, huddled together, listening to speeches as we waited to start our slow march around the White House. A shivering Bill McKibben said he'd waited twenty-five years to see a movement gathered to fight climate change. "And now I've seen it!" he declared. Other environmental and political leaders took the stage; the most moving for me were the indigenous women who together filled the giant screens that projected their images to the crowd. Draped in red with a leather headband, Jackie Thomas, chief and elder of the Saik'uz, one of Canada's First Nations people, told the story of her group's work.

"We formed an alliance to stop the Enbridge Northern Gateway Project, which plans to bring tar sands oil to the coast of British Columbia, which will then be put on tankers to be put on the Asian markets," she explained. She talked about the mysterious cancers killing people who lived near the tar sands and the danger of oil spills. She listed places in the United States and Canada where there had already been dangerous oil accidents: Kalamazoo, Alberta, the Northwest Territories, the Gulf of Mexico. . . .

"We are all connected," she said, reminding us that ranchers depended on the same water as indigenous people. "Enbridge has really brought our communities together in Canada. Never before in my life have I seen white and Native work together before now." The crowd cheered.

"Wow!" said George, turning to me with his white eyebrows raised below his yellow hood. "This is the first time in her life she's seen Native people and white people working together!"

"Thank you, Enbridge, for doing this work for me," continued Thomas, and the crowd laughed. As she concluded she reiterated, "For the first time in my life I feel like there is support of many. We can stand before big oil. Not just for my people but for your people."

The connection of all life, human and animal, ran through the speeches of the First Nations women, who spoke of their obligation to their children, their ancestors, and to their "one true mother." It seemed so simple, so obvious, that we humans were interdependent, finding our humanity in each other, as well as our survival. Of course, we all drank the same water. Later, after the march, I would learn that the fight against Keystone had launched a Cowboy Indian Alliance along the pipeline's route, reminding me of the South African alliance against fracking. I would learn of other places, too, where small numbers of historic adversaries were recognizing that their common interests outweighed that which divided them. I would plant my hope in these stories.

This vision of human beings recognizing our universal Oneness would, in the coming years, inspire me to become a vegetarian to reduce my carbon footprint, a sacrifice that felt much easier once I was living in hope rather than despair. It would motivate me to keep speaking about climate change in Africa and keep organizing. In just over a year, I would be one of the main planners and trainers of the action that led to my second arrest, where even police joined in a silent prayer for all our children's future. I would continue growing alongside EQAT and the wider movement, which less than two years after the cold Forward on Climate march, would gather ten times the crowd in the streets of Manhattan, with indigenous people from around the world leading the march.

But that was all in the future. Standing in the bitter, February wind between sixteen-year-old Megan and seventy-five-year-old George, I remembered George's comment, "We need to have the experience of being the many," and realized that was part of what had changed for me over the course of the past year. When I'd cried in my three-story house the previous winter, I had felt alone. Now I didn't. I knew I was part of the many, connected to a spiritual force greater than ourselves.

From Africa, to Appalachia, to Alberta, and right around the world, there were ordinary people stepping up to defend the future. Like the crowd that encircled the White House that February day, we were pouring forth—past the view of the Lincoln Memorial, where Martin Luther King, Jr. had spoken at the 1963 March on Washington, past the White House gate where Alice Paul had stood for women's rights, past the wrought iron fence where I had stood a few days before. We were the many, emboldened by the realization we were not alone, and we were moving forward with hope.

Acknowledgments

I'm very aware that more people have shaped my life than made it into this story, which like any memoir focuses on one strand of a richer tapestry. Although most are not named here, I am grateful for all my friends, family members, teachers, fellow writers, activists, and spiritual companions.

Special thanks go to Deb Valentine and the women of Wordspace who listened patiently as this project evolved. Hilary Beard, my coffee shop buddy and writing role model, encouraged me to work harder, for which I'm very grateful. Gratitude also to the many friends who read a whole draft at some point in the writing process: Stephany Evans, Amey Hutchins, Melissa Klein, Hollister Knowlton, Jennifer Matesa, Carolyn McCoy, Maureen Murphy, Ginney Haas Pauly, Eleanor Stanford, and Lorraine Truten.

Although my old journals, letters, and calendars often helped to flesh out my recollections, writing this book has made me appreciate how imperfect memory can be. I'm grateful to those who read pieces of the manuscript in order to fact-check my stories and historical summaries: Jim Antal, Fiona Burtt, Steve Chase, Mark Eckhert, Doug Gwyn, Zach Hershman, Walter Hjelt Sullivan, Daniel Hunter, Joshua Kahn Russell, George Lakey, Ingrid Lakey, Harlan Pruden, Glen Retief, Marian Ronan, Stanley Sello, Brian Smith, Kaz Uyehara, Deb Valentine, and Tom Volkert. Of course, any mistakes of fact, memory, or interpretation are ultimately mine.

Many thanks to Brooke Warner—coach, editor, and publisher of She Writes Press—for all she does to help women tell their stories, including this one. Thanks also to Cait Levin and Wayne Parrish, who was a quick student of Setswana, as well as Crystal Patriarche and the BookSparks team.

There would have been no story to tell if it weren't for the people of Bobonong, especially Mmadithapelo Ditirwa, who taught me to *bule-disa*, shepherded me around Botswana on my return, and consulted on this project via Skype. Thanks also to Claudia Vesterby and Alexandra Drobac Diagne for encouraging me to go back to Africa, and to the many people who made the trip smooth, especially Fiona Burtt, Kovin Naidoo, Kumi Naidoo, Stanley Sello, and the Rahubes.

Deep gratitude to the growing number of people around the world who are committed to helping humanity change course, especially Bill McKibben, for his vision that we could build a mass movement, and Earth Quaker Action Team, for helping me find my place in it. Tom Volkert has held down the home front through many an EQAT meeting, the two-week trip to southern Africa, and a few arrests. I'm grateful every day for his love and support.

Finally, this book is dedicated to Megan, Luke, Mopati, and Tshego, for though they have never met, they share the future.

Bibliography

Adams, Katherine H. and Michael L. Keene. *Alice Paul and the American Suffrage Campaign*. Champaign, IL: University of Illinois Press, 2007.

Associated Press. "As Arctic Sea Ice Melts, Experts Expect New Low." *The New York Times*, August 27, 2008. http://www.nytimes.com/2008/08/28/science/earth/28seaice.html?_r=2&.

Buechner, Frederick. *Wishful Thinking: A Seeker's ABC*. San Francisco, CA: HarperSanFrancisco, 1993.

Carson, Rachel. *Silent Spring. Fortieth Anniversary Edition*. New York, NY: Houghton Mifflin, 2002.

Duffy, Peter. *The Killing of Major Denis Mahon: A Mystery of Old Ireland*. New York, NY: HarperCollins Publisher, 2007.

Ferris, Amy. *Marrying George Clooney: Confessions from a Midlife Crisis*. Berkeley, CA: Seal Press, 2009.

Friedan, Betty. *The Feminine Mystique*. New York, NY: W. W. Norton & Company, Inc., 1963.

Gardner, Daniel. *The Science of Fear: How the Culture of Fear Manipulates Your Brain*. New York, NY: Penguin Group (Dutton), 2008.

Hertsgaard, Mark. *Hot: Living Through the Next Fifty Years on Earth*. New York, NY: Houghton Mifflin Harcourt Publishing Company, 2011.

Hunter, Daniel. *Strategy and Soul: A Campaigner's Tale of Fighting Billionaires, Corrupt Officials, and Philadelphia Casinos*. Philadelphia, PA: Hyrax Books, 2013.

Keneally, Thomas. *Three Famines: Starvation and Politics*. New York, NY: PublicAffairs (a member of the Perseus Books Group), 2011.

Kidd, Sue Monk. *When the Heart Waits: Spiritual Direction for Life's Sacred Questions*. San Francisco, CA: HarperSanFrancisco, 1992.

Klein, Naomi. Interview with Jason Mark. *Earth Island Journal*, Autumn 2013. http://www.earthisland.org/journal/index.php/eij/article/naomi_klein/.

Kumar, Satish and Freddie Whitefield, eds. *Visionaries: The 20th Century's 100 Most Inspirational Leaders*. White River Junction, VT: Chelsea Green Publishing, 2007.

Lakey, George. *Toward a Living Revolution*. London: Peace News Press, 2012.

Lamott, Anne. *Help, Thanks, Wow: The Three Essential Prayers*. New York: NY: Penguin Group (Riverhead), 2012.

Mandela, Nelson. *Long Walk to Freedom*. New York, NY: Back Bay Books (imprint of Little Brown & Co.), 1995.

McKibben, Bill. *The End of Nature*. New York, NY: Anchor Books (a division of Random House), 1989.

—. Interview with Alexis Adams. *The Sun*, October 2006, Issue 370. http://thesunmagazine.org/issues/370/dream_a_little_dream?print=all.

New American Standard Bible.

O'Dwyer, Philip, "The Irish and Substance Abuse." In Shulamith Straussner, Editor. *Ethnocultural Factors in Substance Abuse Treatment*. New York, NY: The Guildford Press, 2001.

Scheper-Hughes, Nancy. *Saints, Scholars, and Schizophrenics: Mental Illness in Rural Ireland, Twentieth Anniversary Edition*. Berkeley, CA: University of California Press, 2001.

Thoreau, Henry David. *Walden; or, Life in the Woods*. Boston, MA: Tricknor and Fields, 1854.

Wolf, Naomi. *The Beauty Myth: How Images of Beauty Are Used Against Women*. New York, NY: Perennial (a division of HarperCollins Publisher), 2002.

About the Author

© Conrad Louis-Charles

A graduate of both Duke and Yale, Eileen Flanagan writes for a wide range of national publications and speaks at conferences, colleges, and religious gatherings. Her book *The Wisdom to Know the Difference: When to Make a Change—and When to Let Go* was endorsed by the Dalai Lama and won a Silver Nautilus Book Award. She lives with her husband and two children in Philadelphia, where she serves as clerk of the board of Earth Quaker Action Team. Learn more about her work at www.eileenflanagan.com.

SELECTED TITLES FROM SHE WRITES PRESS

She Writes Press is an independent publishing company
founded to serve women writers everywhere.
Visit us at www.shewritespress.com.

100 Under $100: One Hundred Tools for Empowering Global Women
by Betsy Teutsch $29.95, 978-1-63152-934-4
An inspiring, comprehensive look at the many tools being employed today
to empower women in the developing world and help them raise themselves out of poverty.

Seeing Red: A Woman's Quest for Truth, Power, and the Sacred by Lone Morch
$16.95, 978-1-938314-12-4
One woman's journey over inner and outer mountains—a quest that takes
her to the holy Mt. Kailas in Tibet, through a seven-year marriage, and
into the arms of the fierce goddess Kali, where she discovers her powerful,
feminine self.

The Outskirts of Hope: A Memoir by Jo Ivester
$16.95, 978-1-63152-964-1
A moving, inspirational memoir about how living and working in an all-
black town during the height of the civil rights movement profoundly
affected the author's entire family—and how they in turn impacted the
community.

This is Mexico: Tales of Culture and Other Complications by Carol M. Merchasin
$16.95, 978-1-63152-962-7
Merchasin chronicles her attempts to understand Mexico, her adopted
country, through improbable situations and small moments that keep the
reader moving between laughter and tears.

Where Have I Been All My Life? A Journey Toward Love and Wholeness
by Cheryl Rice $16.95, 978-1-63152-917-7
Rice's universally relatable story of how her mother's sudden death
launched her on a journey into the deepest parts of grief—and, ultimately,
toward love and wholeness.

Loveyoubye: Holding Fast, Letting Go, And Then There's The Dog
by Rossandra White $16.95, 978-1-938314-50-6
A soul-searching memoir detailing the painful, but ultimately liberating,
disintegration of a twenty-five-year marriage.